Narrative Methods for Organizational and Communication Research

'David Boje has emerged as the leading postmodern thinker in management theory and organization science. His prolific output lights the path for others to follow in a field awakening to the challenge of postmodern critical theory. In this new book, Boje takes on the foundational issue of narratives and stories that underlie the sense-making of human experience and theory. Updating and revising narrative theory for the prevailing "postmodern condition", Boje masterfully reconstructs the concepts and methods of storytelling, as he subverts the dominant principles of modernist organization theory. He offers a subtle and complex notion of narrative that belies the fallacies of totalizing and linear approaches, and allows for the full complexity of fragmented, partial, and polyphonic voices and meanings of life to be heard. This impressive book should leave an indelible mark on management and organization studies.'
Steven Best, University of Texas, El Paso

'This book is timely and first rate.'
Thomas Lee, University of Washington

'Boje masterfully shows how to analyze texts and ideas before they are reduced and fitted into the dominant ideological frameworks of the day.'
Paul Hirsch, Northwestern University

SAGE SERIES IN MANAGEMENT RESEARCH

SERIES EDITORS

RICHARD THORPE
Department of Management
Manchester Metropolitan University

MARK EASTERBY-SMITH
Centre for the Study of Management Learning
The Management School, Lancaster University

The Sage Series in Management Research contains concise and accessible texts, written by internationally respected authors, on the theory and practice of management and organisational research. Each volume addresses a particular methodological approach or set of issues, providing the reader with more detailed discussion and analysis than can be found in most general management research texts. These books will be indispensable for academics, research students and managers undertaking research.

Narrative Methods
for Organizational
and Communication Research

David M. Boje

SAGE Publications
London • Thousand Oaks • New Delhi

First published 2001

Apart from any fair dealing for the purposes of research or
private study, or criticism or review, as permitted under the
Copyright, Designs and Patents Act, 1988, this publication
may be reproduced, stored or transmitted in any form, or
by any means, only with the prior permission in writing of
the publishers, or in the case of reprographic reproduction,
in accordance with the terms of licences issued by the
Copyright Licensing Agency. Inquiries concerning
reproduction outside those terms should be sent to the
publishers.

 SAGE Publications Ltd
6 Bonhill Street
London EC2A 4PU

SAGE Publications Inc
2455 Teller Road
Thousand Oaks, California 91320

SAGE Publications India Pvt Ltd
32, M-Block Market
Greater Kailash - I
New Delhi 110 048

British Library Cataloguing in Publication data

A catalogue record for this book
is available from the British Library

ISBN 0 7619 6586 6 hbk
ISBN 0 7619 6587 4 pbk

Library of Congress catalog card number available

Typeset by SIVA Math Setters, Chennai, India
Printed in Great Britain by Athenaeum Press, Gateshead

Contents

Introduction

Overview

Traditionally story has been viewed as less than narrative. Narrative requires plot, as well as coherence. To narrative theory, story is folksy, without emplotment, a simple telling of chronology. I propose 'antenarrative.' Antenarrative is the fragmented, non-linear, incoherent, collective, unplotted and pre-narrative speculation, a bet. To traditional narrative methods antenarrative is an improper storytelling, a wager that a proper narrative can be constituted. Narrative tries to stand as elite, to be above story. The crisis of narrative method in modernity is what to do with non-linear, almost living storytelling that is fragmented, polyphonic (many voiced) and collectively produced. My response is to stretch the traditional approach by including what I call 'antenarrative' methods. The focus is on the analysis of stories that are too unconstructed and fragmented to be analysed in traditional approaches. The postmodern and chaotic soup of storytelling is somewhat difficult to analyse. Stories in organization are self-deconstructing, flowing, emerging and networking, not at all static. The purpose of this book is to set out eight antenarrative analysis options that can deal with the prevalence of fragmented and polyphonic storytelling in complex organizations and to provide teaching examples of these methods that are applicable to organization studies. The analyses to be given an antenarrative reading include deconstruction, grand narrative, microstoria, story networking, intertextuality, causality, plot and theme analysis. Narrative analysis combined with antenarrative analysis can help this field be a more multi-voiced methodology that focuses on non-linear, unplotted storytelling. This fragmented, non-linear, incoherent, collective, unplotted, and improper storytelling, is what I mean by the term *'antenarrative'*.

What is antenarrative?

I give 'antenarrative' a double meaning: as being before and as a bet. First, story is 'ante' to narrative; it is 'antenarrative'. A 'narrative' is something that is narrated, i.e. 'story'. Story is an account of incidents or events, but narrative comes after and adds 'plot' and 'coherence' to the story line. Story is therefore 'ante' to story and narrative is post-story. Story is an 'ante' state of affairs existing previously to narrative; it is in advance of narrative. Used as an adverb, 'ante' combined with 'narrative' means earlier than narrative.

Secondly, ante is a bet, something to do with gambling and speculation. The noun 'ante' has an etymology dating to 1838 that is defined as 'a poker stake usually put up before the deal to build the pot <the dealer called for a dollar ante>' (Merriam-Webster Dictionary). In horse racing, 'ante-post' is a wager made on a horse before that day of the race. As a verb, it is anteing.

Since story, narrative and antenarrative are used throughout the book, some introduction is important. Story resists narrative; story is antenarrative and on occasion even anti-narrative (a refusal to be coherent). The folk of organizations inhabit storytelling spaces outside plot, not tidy and rationalized narrative spaces. Narrative analysts replace folk stories with less messy academic narrative emplotments and create an account of organizations that is fictively rational, free of tangled contingency and against story.

I would therefore disagree with Czarniawska when she says 'a *story* consists of a plot comprising causally related episodes that culminate in a solution to a problem' (1997: 78). To me this is the definition of a *narrative*, not a story. I rely more on Ricoeur's definition of story, as he endorses Gallie's (1968: 22) approach:

> A story describes a sequence of actions and experiences done or undergone by a certain number of people, whether real or imaginary. These people are presented either in situations that change or as reacting to such change. In turn, these changes reveal hidden aspects of the situation and the people involved, and engender a new predicament which calls for thought, action, or both. This response to the new situation leads the story toward its conclusion. (1984: 150)

Even this definition of story has for me too much closure, but the concept of the followability of story allows us to look at antenarration before the emplotment of story, and to search for pre-understanding before the story becomes followable.

Elsewhere Czarniawska defines narrative in a way I agree with, 'For them to become a narrative, they require a *plot*, that is, some way to bring them into a meaningful whole' (1999: 2). I prefer to think of narratives as the theory that organization and other theorists use with stories, to see how narratives and prenarratives are acts of 'commodification, exchange, and consumption' (Clair et al., 1996: 255). 'They are narratives dressed as theory' (Clair, 1998: 20).

To translate story into narrative is to impose counterfeit coherence and order on otherwise fragmented and multi-layered experiences of desire. As Weick puts it 'When people punctuate their own living into stories, they impose a formal coherence on what is otherwise a flowing soup' (1995: 128). White also observes that narrative theory is a finalization that 'transforms events into historical facts by demonstrating their ability to function as elements of completed stories' (1987: 251). Antenarrative is never final; it is improper.

Stories are 'antenarrative' when told without the proper plot sequence and mediated coherence preferred in narrative theory. These are stories that are too unconstructed and fragmented to be captured by retrospective sensemaking. 'The important point', says Weick 'is that retrospective sensemaking is an activity in which many possible meanings may need to be synthesized, because many different projects [stories] are under way at the time reflection takes place' (1995: 27, additions mine). There is an implicit bet that such retrospective form may emerge, but it does not always take place. More sensemaking keeps displacing closure.

Antenarrative is not the same as 'anti'-narrative. In anti-narrative, the person cannot narrate plot or closure, but is in the present moment. This occurs in the telling of a personal experience story, for example Nancy whose mother has Alzheimer's:

> And if I'm trying to get dinner ready and I'm already feeling bad, she's in front of the refrigerator. Then she goes to put her hand on the stove and I got the fire on. And then she's in front of the microwave and then she's in front of the silverware drawer. And – and if I send her out she gets mad at me. And then it's awful. That's when I have a really, a really bad time. (Charmaz, 1991: 173 as cited in Frank, 1995: 99)

The nominal glue of Alzheimer's binds the story fragments together in a Baldessari-like anti-narrative. 'One can conceive of "anti-narratives" whose storytelling purpose is precisely not only to deny any overall meaning or plot (as telos or process) but to display fragmentation, discontinuities, partial and temporary understandings, and the lack of fixed meanings while equally claiming to mimic or evoke the nature of the past world as experienced' (Pluciennik et al., 1999: 653). Anti-narrative and antenarrative do share this in common: both are beyond the closure required of narrative theory. Next, I will introduce some definitions of antenarrative.

Five dimensions of antenarrative

First, antenarrating is both before whatever narratology as a method and theory supplements, frames and imposes onto story. This is often the requirement for a beginning, middle and end, complete with a moral and an agreed plot. There is a double sense of 'ante' as 'being before' narrative and as still a 'speculation' that I think returns something important to storytelling, or what I will call 'antenarrating'.

Secondly, antenarrative gives attention to the speculative, the ambiguity of sensemaking and guessing as to what is happening in the flow of experience. It answers the question 'what is going on here?'. Antenarrative is constituted out of the flow of lived experience, while narrative method is more meta; it is about the storytelling that came before. Narrative is post, a retrospective explanation of storytelling's speculative appreciations. Narrative is a form of memory of the story, but I think none that omits the antenarrative speculation, about what Shutz calls 'coming-to-be' (see Weick, 1995: 25). It is the speculative that gets lost in the narrative method focus on taxonomy, plot and coherence; the sense made becomes too bounded and overdetermined.

Thirdly, antenarrative directs our analytic attention to the flow of story-telling, as a sensemaking to lived experience before the narrative require-ments of beginnings, middles or endings. Narrative theory is an experience of the after-effects of storytelling once coherence is rendered, while ante-narrative is an experience of the storytelling life with abbreviated and interrupted story performances that yield plurivocality (Boje, 1995). And that life has its rules. 'There are implicit rules in storytelling (who can tell it, to whom, and where)' (Boje, 1991: 124). Clair adds the rule of *how*, 'organi-zational members tell their stories. *How* organizational members frame their experiences and accounts may severely impact the kind and amount of exposure the story will receive' (1998: 74).

Fourthly, antenarrative is about the Tamara of storytelling (Boje, 1995). In *Tamara*, Los Angeles' longest-running play, a dozen characters unfold their stories before a walking, sometimes running, audience. They are try-ing to find out 'who done it?'. Instead of remaining stationary, viewing a single stage, the audience fragments into small groups that chase charac-ters from one room to the next, from one floor to the next, even going into bedrooms, kitchens and other chambers to chase and co-create the stories that interest them the most. If there are a dozen stages and a dozen story-tellers, the number of story lines an audience could trace as it chases the wandering discourses of *Tamara* is 12 factorial (479,001,600).

To me Tamara is a way to describe how storytelling as antenarrative occurs in complex organizations. It is before narrative closure; it is specu-lative, and it is in the flow of experience. The Tamara antenarrative specu-lation highlights the plurivocal interpretation of organizational stories in a distributed and historically contextualized meaning network – that is, the meaning of events depends upon the locality, the prior sequence of stories and the transformation of characters in the wandering discourses.

Tamara is also the basis of an antenarrative theory of storytelling organi-zations. In storytelling organizations, as seen in *Tamara*, a wandering linguistic framework exists in which stories are the medium of interpre-tative exchange. Storytelling organizations are antenarrative, existing to tell their collective stories, to live out their collective stories, to be in con-stant struggle over getting the stories of insiders and outsiders straight. It is a sensemaking that is coming into being, but not finished or concluded, in narrative retrospection.

Fifthly, antenarrative is collective memory before it becomes reified into the story, the consensual narrative. It is before the plots have been agreed to; it is still in a state of coming-to-be, still in flux. As Weick puts it 'actions are known only when they have been completed' (1995: 26). And narra-tives are known after they have been completely analysed. I am more interested in antenarrative, where people are still chasing stories, and many different logics for plotting an ongoing event are still being investigated. Gephart (1992: 119–21), for example, did a study of a serious accident, and noted how the logic of top-management differed from that of the operators. And because people in organizations typically are chasing multiple story lines and are aware that overdetermining the story is risky, the collective memory is always being reworked and worked out, but never completed. It is reflection that is under way, not, as Weick says, 'because it makes no sense at all, but because it makes many different kinds of sense' (1995: 27). In collective memory, some story sensing contradicts others, and working it out is the stuff of antenarrative.

Postmodern antenarratives
The postmodern condition of fragmentation and simulation makes coherence problematic. There is no whole story to tell, only fragments, which even with retrospective sensemaking cannot find a plot that will make the fragments cohere. Instead a wandering audience chases storylines on multiple and simultaneous stages. In such a Tamara of collective sensemaking, people are only tracing story fragments, inventing bits and pieces to glue it all together, but never able to visit all the stages and see the whole. In the radical postmodern antenarrative, organization characters collide rather than interact, as to come in and out of one another's theatrical stages. And there is for each person a Tamara of stages, happening simultaneously, and we do not get to participate in all the performances. Rather than reified plots, there are fragments of stories, bits and pieces told here and there, to varying audiences, so that no one knows a whole story and there are no whole stories anyway. And pockets of some agreement come undone. There are occasionally coherent plots, but elsewhere only jagged edges and bottomless pits of chaos to tiptoe around. In such Tamara, the demand to narrate the whole is met by long periods of silence.

In the personal experience narration, the storyteller and narrator are one. In all other narratives, someone else tells the story and makes it into a formal narrative, one with mediated coherence and plot. But, in the Tamara of many story involvements with so many story fragments, coherence and plot are hard to come by. In formal narration, there is a (linear) plot and a mediated coherence provided by the narrator. To narrative theory, story is folksy, without emplotment, a simple telling of chronology. But people live in the antenarrative. Narrative adds the plot and tries to stand as elite above story as antenarrative. The crisis of narrative in modernity is what to do with non-linear storytelling, with fragmented and polyphonic (many voiced) stories, the Tamara of collective story production, and the everyday storyteller immersed in fragmentation. Stories are antenarrative and everywhere in organizations, and are somewhat difficult to analyse. People are always in the middle of living and tracing their storied lives.

According to TwoTrees (1997), stories have three properties: time, place and mind. I believe that many narratologies currently being applied in the field of organizational analysis and the social sciences more broadly marginalize these three properties. In effect, narratology marginalizes *story*. In what follows, I will critically review common narratologies and suggest some ways in which the idea of story can be returned to analysis.

Stories, TwoTrees (1997) suggests, have:

1. A *time*, 'You tell a story at a certain time of the year, a season, or time of the day. There are Fall and Spring stories.'
2. A *place*, 'You recount stories at this place, and places have their own story.'
3. A *mind*, 'Every creation, even a story, has a life of its own. We create a story and it has a life. The stories have origins. You must tell a story with permission.'

For TwoTrees, stories must be re-contextualized back to their time, place and mind. The stories live and there are penalties for getting a story wrong or telling it without permission. 'What is the Lakota penalty for changing a story, telling a story wrong or without permission?' David Boje asked at a presentation by TwoTrees. 'It is death,' she replied. Why death? 'Because, the story in an oral culture is the entire living history of the community' (TwoTrees, 1997).

The purpose of this book is to set out eight antenarrative analysis options that can deal with the prevalence of fragmented and polyphonic storytelling in complex organizations. The order of alternative narrative analyses is:

1. deconstruction
2. grand narrative
3. microstoria
4. story network
5. intertextuality
6. causality
7. plot and
8. theme.

On the duality of narratives and stories

Reviewing the structuralist traditions of Russian Formalists (Propp and Shklovsky), American structuralism (James, Lubbock, Booth and Chatman), and French Structuralists (Barthes, Todorov, Bremond, Greimas, Pavel and Prince) Jonathan Culler identifies a duality of narrative over story, noting: 'if these theorists agree on anything it is this: that the theory of narrative requires a distinction between what I shall call "story" – a sequence of actions or events, conceived as independent of their manifestation in discourse – and what I shall call "discourse," the discursive presentation or narration of events' (1981: 169).

There can be several narrators to a story. Someone who lived through an experience can offer his/her 'personal experience narrative'. They tell their own story. Ricoeur summarizes Gallie's (1968: 22) story definition as follows:

A story describes a sequence of actions and experiences done or undergone by a certain number of people, whether real or imaginary. These people are presented either in situations that change or as reacting to such change. In turn, these changes reveal hidden aspects of the situation and the people involved, and engender a new predicament which calls for thought, action, or both. This response to the new situation leads the story toward its conclusion. (1984: 150)

Storytellers own the rights to narrate, and sorting these story rights is a constant occupation of organizational participants. But, when someone else tells a story s/he did not inhabit, it is a different type of narrating. Researchers, even ethnographers, who live in the field, narrate differently than those who live their story. Some say story is mere chronology while narration is what sociologists, historians, anthropologists and other social scientists do. Yet, as Lyotard (1979/1984) made abundantly clear, scientists tell stories about their data and use story to sell their theory. Gephart's (1988) ethnostatistics are proof enough that narrating and rhetoric go on in the statistical work of social science. A statistical formula and the explanation of a table of equations can be considered forms of narrative. McCloskey (1998) is convinced that economists narrate and use rhetoric that they do not want an answer to.

What is the hegemony of narrative?
Some people are not ready to narrate their story. They are approached by social scientists and invited, even required to narrate. As someone narrates an experience for the first time, a retrospective sensemaking can occur as chaotic experience is given narrative order. But sensemaking is not all there is. Some experiences lack that linear sequence and are difficult to tell as a 'coherent' story. Telling stories that lack coherence is contrary to modernity. Yet in the postmodern condition, stories are harder to tell because experience itself is so fragmented and full of chaos that fixing meaning or imagining coherence is fictive. Other stories are hard to tell because whatever meaning there may be has not been reflected upon, and there is a lack of distance and perspective. Death, divorce and disease stories are hard to narrate. One can only trace the edges of the wounds. There are experiences that are just too shattering to put into words, too fantastic to narrate. 'Lived chaos makes reflection, and consequently story-telling, impossible' (Frank, 1995: 98).

We are said to be *homo fabulans*, humans telling and interpreting narratives. But there is always more to a good story. For Polkinghorne (1988) narrative analysis is defined by a very pragmatic insight, all inquiry is a process of narrative negotiations. In the narrative negotiations between qualitative researchers and the folk, the folk are not doing too well, their phenomenal experience is reduced to readable and 'proper' narrative. The purpose of the book is to provide counter-examples of dominant paradigms of narrative interpretation and analysis so that fewer stories will get reduced to narrative models. I seek to improve the narrative of organizations by recovering the polyphonic qualities of its storytellers. I long for a different storytelling, a collective storytelling that is antenarrative and undoes the linear time frames of modernity; I bet on the incoherent and the unplotted tellings.

Multi-story
In the dominant paradigms of (monological) narrative analysis in organization studies, multi-story is defined as noise, or a sequential or simplistic chronological case study that needs analysis to make it narrate. Story is viewed as antenarrative (just chronicle). The game in academia is to create a narrative from so many stories, and retell the narrative not the stories in academic circles. My narrative negotiation is subversive. I seek to negotiate a new relation between narrative and story (antenarrative). Narrative knowing must include those ways of antenarrative analysis of stories told in organizational communities in which the telling of stories is the currency of knowledge making and knowledge negotiation.

All the chapter titles in this book are not new, but are rendered with new slants. My hope is that by making these alternative narrative analyses of stories more accessible with concise chapters, this will invite others to conduct these methods and soon 'microstoria', 'intertextuality' and 'narrative causality' will be as popular as the Harvard Case study. Or better yet, cases will be rewritten into more polyvocal tapestries.

Narrated cases
I read one study that said narrative analysis is nearly the same thing as the Harvard Case study. To me this is a ridiculous assertion, justification to write a one-voiced and homogeneous way of narrating where the omniscient narrator hides behind every line. Often, someone else's story is what gets analysed and that can be a more coherent and ordered plot than the teller imagined. And how do these cases read? In the classroom, unlike the unprocessed 'story' the formal case study reconstructs and replaces 'stories' of the flux of experience with a 'narrative' plot and a 'moral' to be comprehended as a sequential whole. Narrative then has a closer correlation with coherent structure and the emplotment of causal explanation than does the less elegant 'story'. Yet the case study is an account prenarrated to trap students into obvious endings.

To go beyond the overused case approaches, be they comparative, functionalist or structuralist raises an important challenge. Cases, dare I say are 'elitist' protocols that disparage and ridicule the ill-formed and fragmented non-retrospective story. I have collected together eight alternative narrative analyses that I contend are equally applicable to organization studies of 'story', but not so widely used as case approaches. Avoiding these alternative narrative ways of telling and interpreting stories I would argue posits characters, events, plots and accounts that are not merely a chronicle or even a collection of stories to which an analysis can be applied. A universal analysis of major and minor factors and voices. What else can a progressive and romantic narrative unfold? Enter discourse analysis with its non-method deconstructions. If students get beyond complex intellectual models with bizarre language, it is a great way to teach students to think critically. Yet the deconstruction of romantic cases into themes of tragedy and hegemony, with a prolonged stare into the abyss, is not so popular in the classroom.

How does a field that centres on profoundly narrative, case study knowing resituate itself as an academic knowledge-making enterprise amid other postmodern storytelling that is fairly antenarrative in epistemological stance? Harvard cases are just the surface issue in narrating organizations differently. I decided to focus on alternative analyses since so much of what passes for academic narrative analysis in organization studies seems to rely upon sequential, single-voiced stories. In short, it is an excessive reliance on the hypothetical-deductive approach. I do a fair share of narrative reviews for journals and I see too many manuscripts that contain one-shot interviews, content analysis and taxonomy that result in largely shallow examinations. In narrative analyses we need to do more than treat stories as 'in-place metering' devices to measure more important constructs like culture, tacit knowledge or knowledge work. Beyond sequential and single-voiced case study and one-sided interviews, we can conceive of non-linear and even antenarrative accounts of experience and disputations of collective memory. This would then accomplish my goal, to improve the narrative of organizations.

How to tell organization stories differently
Narrative analysis combined with antenarrative analysis can be a field that is about multi-voiced ways of telling stories, with even antenarrative and non-linear ones whose linear plot sequence is missing and where no one seems to mind. To tell organization stories differently will, I think, require this more dialectic approach. But narrating what? Other ways to story 'Others' who refuse to narrate? I call to enact alternative narrative analyses that will story 'Others' and the author. This can yield new narratives in organization studies, ones that are multi-voiced, rich with fragmentation and lacking in linearity. Even antenarrative in the sense that the reader is free to put the fragments together or just leave the narrative wreckage where it lies.

Qualitative researchers have discussed the implications of using plots in research reports that map and embed specific epistemological, political, methodological or other affiliations (e.g. Geertz, 1973, 1988; Herndl, 1993; Van Maanen, 1988).

The alternative ways I assembled focus on multi-stranded stories of experiences that lack collective consensus. I seek alternatives to the fiat of the single-voiced, single-authored narrative dictating organization memory. For example, we will look at intertextuality as a way to explore multi-stranded stories, and microstoria to examine stories of the 'little people' telling many histories that were omitted from the conquering hero or even

Table 1.1 *Antenarrative approaches*

1. Deconstruction	It is antenarrative in action, in ongoing acts of narrative self-deconstruction. The narrative is not fixed, but moves and flows with networks of embedded meaning. The analyst joins in the antenarrative by becoming part of the ongoing textual deconstruction of interpenetrating processes and weaves of reconstructing, unravelling and constructing stories.
2. Grand narrative	It is antenarrative in how one story can be told in ways that erase a prior way of telling the story. The ambition is to shatter grand narrative into many small stories and to problematize any linear mono-voiced grand narrative of the past by replacing it with an open polysemous (many-meanings) and multivocal (many-voiced) web of little stories. Not everyone wants grand narratives banished, which gives the tension between dominant or grand narrative, and the ante-narrating of little stories.
3. Microstoria	Antenarrative because they are quite against the narrating in deconstruction, postmodern, grounded theory, and macro-history. They prefer to situate their 'little' story approach in Peircean 'abduction' (abduction stands between induction and deduction). They prefer local antenarrative knowledge, the 'little people's' histories and seem to ignore the macro narrative 'great man' accounts that are so fashionable in organization studies. Finally they resist interpreting 'little' people's stories of times long past into contemporary modern or postmodern narrative fashion.
4. Story network	Stories can become nodes or links in a narrative network analysis, mere architectural display. By contrast, in antenarrative analysis the analyst traces the storytelling behaviour in the organizing situation. The organization is seen as a storytelling system in which stories are the medium of exchange. Antenarrative focuses on the ground that moves not on the map and analytic portrayal.
5. Intertextuality	It posits its own antenarrative network, a dialogic conversation among writers and readers of texts. Intertextuality gets at the process issues that narrative network analysis seems to miss. Intertext is a plurality, the polyphony of voices, a veritable textual system that is stereographic and almost living to use Barthes images.
6. Causality	The antenarrative alternative is to study situated acts of storytelling that retrospectively erect and re-erect causality attributions. The causal field is messy and often unfathomable, and acts of narration camouflage the antenarrative fabric. To study the non-linear antenarrative pathways of story reconstruction before retrospective sensemaking is an alternative to causal map methodology.
7. Plot	Plot analysis is based in Ricoeur's theory of *emplotment*, which allows for conditions of antenarrative, such as when there is not sufficient pre-understanding or coherence to grasp together a plot. Relevant to organization studies are questions of who gets to author the narrative in emplotments of complex organizations and what other emplotments are feasible?

(contd.)

Table 1.1 (contd.)

8.	Theme	An antenarrative approach to theme is opposed to taxonomic classification. Taxonomy cells are little narrative cells to trap stories. Antenarrative cannot be caged in taxonomy or the hierarchy of classification. Antenarrative highlights the storytelling moves and flows beyond such limits. Theme analysis would divest story of time, place, plurality and connectivity. Theme and taxonomy from an antenarrative view are a terrorist discourse, an analysis reduced to stereotypes, and a foreclosure on storytelling polysemy and a degradation of living exchange. It is the excess and in-between of theme analysis that concerns us here. Beyond the logic of theme the cells of taxonomy are the messy plenitude. Antenarrative theme analysis steps outside containment to engage fragmentation, becoming and undoing.

the bourgeoisie CEO's account. Intertextual and microstoria analyses are contrary to grand narratives of great heroes or grand projects. Each chapter will consist of these different analyses and present applications including examples of stories and analysis.

The book is intended for researchers wanting to do narrative analysis differently. It is a book that can be used in graduate seminars in several disciplines to supplement 'standard' methods of narrative analysis. Narrative analysis spans organization research in business, sociology, ecology and communication disciplines. Yet, if the narrative analysis is only a search for coherent, linear and ordered tales, as told by narrative authorities, then the stories written about organizations are too shallow and superficial, and cover more than they tell. Van Maanen (1988) calls them 'realist' tales of the field. Beginning graduate students who want to know how to conduct specific types of qualitative story analysis can use this book. But they may want to start with a more standard text if they are searching for 'realist' tales, and yet, some of the narrative analyses I seek to explore and make accessible to students are about the 'materiality' of narrative.

There are many other viable analyses that did not make my list. I value greatly, for example, the life history work of George Roth, but George has skillfully rendered this already. There is also the ethnostatistics narrative work of Robert Gephart Jr. Here again, he has masterfully presented the approach elsewhere. I also did not put in work on narrative ethnography. That training is available in anthropology seminars and in English and Communication too. The alternatives I present are very much a part of these broader discourses.

My focus is on rendering approaches that are as yet not accessible to the qualitative methods classroom or to the journals of organization studies. The book begins and ends with approaches that are not new, but what is new is the alternative (antenarrative) reading given to each. Table 1.1 provides an overview of the antenarrative stance of each chapter.

The chapters

Chapter 1, **Deconstruction**, is not new. Beginning with deconstruction allows us to immediately challenge ideas of telos, linearity, sequence, voice and plot. I shall approach deconstruction as something that is happening in the ongoing acts of self-deconstruction in the systemic nature of narratives, in the dynamic weave of differences within and between texts, that always seem to be unravelling their embedded (inter)textual networks of thought. My deconstruction view is antenarrative, since texts are self-deconstructing without the help of the analyst. Moreover, the role of the analyst is always part of the antenarrative experience and connects to deconstruction. What is new here is the examination of differences between outright destruction and what I read as deconstruction, and the call to resituate the dualities and hierarchies that get unpacked.

In Chapter 2, **Grand narrative**, made so (in)famous by Lyotard (1984) is also not new, but is certainly antenarrative. It is antenarrative in how one story can be told in ways that erase a prior way of telling the story. The ambition is to shatter grand narrative and to problematize any linear mono-voiced grand narrative of the past by replacing it with an open poly-semous (many meanings) and multivocal (many-voiced) web of little stories. Modernist organizational science is presented as a linear grand narrative, where postmodern science stresses the nonlinear, multi-vocality and impressionistic fragmentation of knowledge. While not new, grand narrative studies are still rare in organization studies. For instance, Lyotard is incredulous to the grand narratives. However, saying it does not make it so. Moreover, to reject all grand narrative, I shall argue, does not seem to be too wise. The alternative that is offered in this book is to look at the interplay of grand and local narration. The grand narratives of modernity, such as McDonalds and Marketeers, suggest not everyone wants grand narratives banished.

Microstoria, as approached in Chapter 3, is to me a unique antenarrative alternative to the narrative analyses done so abundantly in organization studies. It is also quite a contrast to grand narrative or the universality of macrohistory. For this reason, I situate the microstorian approach here. Microstorians I have read are quite against deconstruction, post-modern and grounded theory, and prefer to situate their approach in Peircean 'abduction' (abduction stands between induction and deduction). Microstorians are not postmodern since they do not see texts as free-floating webs of signifiers or as schizophrenic narratives. They do not surrender notions of textual materiality, nor do they abandon class and are not so eager to dismiss all grand narrative. They are antenarrative because they look to 'little' acts of resistance to dominant narratives. They also reject conditioning or framing narratives of the past by contemporary theories of the present. Microstorians do prefer local knowledge, the 'little people's' histories and seem to ignore the 'great man' accounts that are so fashionable in organization studies. Microstoria relies on archival records and these analysts are at times quite material and empirical in ways that textual deconstruction is not. They claim not to be too aligned with grounded theory or with the genealogy of Foucault. Rather, they aspire to the adduction middle ground between deductive and inductive analysis.

Story network analysis is positioned in Chapter 4 since the microstorians do name searches in their archival research to fashion name networks. Story networks are becoming all the narrative rage with aggregated causal mapping and latticed taxonomic architecture among story bits. But they are not being done with the kind of attention to context that is the stock and trade of the microstorians. The alternative I offer is more of an embedded antenarrative process focus to network analysis. I point out the dangers more than celebrate the accomplishments of story networks. The weakness of story network analysis is its overdetermination of structure, as opposed to processes of collective memory and social dynamics. What is the antenarrative alternative? Microstorians use story network analysis in an antenarrative sense by tracing the names of 'little people' and their social relations (family and economic) to other people. In story network analysis, one collects layers of embedded storied relationships. Or, one collects stories and traces their relationship (person) links in the *in situ* and contextualized processes. Stories can become nodes or links in a narrative network analysis, but in antenarrative analysis the analyst traces the storytelling behaviour in the organizing situation. What the analyst narrates are the deductively derived taxonomies that show the associations among story types (nodes). I have seen these studies presented to journal reviewers as grounded theory.

Intertextuality is not new, but where are the organization studies? It is rarely, if ever applied in organization research and yet each day organizations add more texts to an intertextual world. Intertextuality gets at the process issues that narrative network analysis seems to miss. So this is why I situate it in Chapter 5. Intertextuality posits its own antenarrative network, a dialogic conversation among writers and readers of texts. Intertextuality is all the dialoguing that goes on between and within narratives. Intertextuality is explored quite fruitfully in Fairclough's work, but ignored is the element that was so important to Kristeva, the carnival. When modernity freed itself of the monologic and single-voiced author, the carnivalesque was released with the force of the polyphonic novel. And this polyphonic narrating and intertextuality continue to excite postmodern sensibility. In intertextual analysis we look for a crowd of authors, actors and readers engaged in carnivalesque scenes of dynamic textual production, distribution and consumption.

Causality analysis, Chapter 6, begins with Nietzsche's theory of causality. Causality precedes Chapter 7, plot, which has as its element, causality. By definition a narrative explains the 'why': what caused a series of events or phenomena to happen, unfold and end the way they did? The standard narrative causality analysis is to inventory narrative for causal assertions in texts and then erect a taxonomy or a set of abstracted and aggregated causal maps. But as Nietzsche (1956/1987) reminds, 'causality alludes us' and is no more than an 'invention', a way of plotting events. In this sense, the causality analysis I propose is an antenarrative one. I am interested in recovering an antenarrative causality, the acts of storytelling that construct and reconstruct causality. Calling the causal narration of organizing into question is an antenarrative analysis. The causal field is messy and often unfathomable and acts of narration destroy the antenarrative fabric. In the postmodern world of organizations linear causality is a convenient fiction, an over-simplified narrative of complex antenarrative dynamics in which non-linearity (and that too is a fiction) reigns.

Plot analysis is older than Aristotle is. The antenarrative analysis alternative I present in Chapter 7 builds upon Ricoeur's work on the mimetics of emplotment. Relevant to organization studies are questions of who gets to author the narrative in emplotments of complex organizations and what other emplotments are feasible? There are also questions of how to bring the writers and readers of plot into intertextual dialogue. Ricoeur (1984) argues that readers cannot follow a story plot through its twists, turns, contingencies, coincidences and dead ends to a foregone narrative conclusion without a great deal of pre-understanding and that followability can be analysed in a structural model inter-relating time and narrative coherence.

Finally, we reach narrative **theme analysis** and the end of our journey in Chapter 8. Theme analysis is old, but the inductive enquiries are much rarer than the deductive taxonomies. While theme analysis has been done before, what is at issue is the relationship between deductive, inductive and antenarrative analysis. Do we impose etic (outsider) taxonomies of narratives or do we engage in etic (insider) dialogue to become aware of how people experience narratives? In either case, the narrative analysis can be limiting when the relationships between the cells and the excess beyond the taxonomy are not explored. This exploration for me takes place with antenarrative. Theme analysis is the last chapter because it is common to almost all qualitative work, and to change it in any way is a daunting task.

In Chapter 8, I will take several etic categories of narrative themes: bureaucratic, quest, chaos and postmodern as our starting point. I will then look at the etic fabrication and the emic experience of each one, as well as the antenarrative ebb and flow of stories outside and between these types. I will then resituate the etic/emic duality by showing how one bleeds into the other. This is not new: I will show, for example, how we learn our etic frames in school and how analysts trip over emic frames and then after writing them out, erase all the emic authors of the narrative. But this is not the contribution I seek to make.

An antenarrative approach to theme moves beyond theme and sub-theme taxonomic classification. Taxonomy in narrative theme analysis traps stories in little cells. Antenarrative does not destroy the cell house of

Table 1.2 *Narratologies*

Narratology	Ontology	Epistemology	Methodology
Living story	Stories live and possess time, place and mind.	Knowledge is the story performed in time, place and has a life of its own (mind); story cannot be dualized from context without imbalance and other consequences.	Restory the relation between dominant narrative and authors' preferred story.
Realist Peters and Waterman (1982) Hammer and Champy (1993); Harvard cases	'Real' reality mirrored more or less imperfectly in narrative or case. Narrative is a cultural artefact and object; social facts.	Dualist: real is real, narrative is subjective interpretive knowledge; story is an object to know other objects (culture, etc.); managerialist; strategic.	Experimental manipulation; interview with narrative as measures; narrate with rating scales; biography of narrative uniqueness.
Formalist Barthes (early) Ricoeur Levi-Strauss Propp Shklovsky Fisher Frye de Saussure H. White	'Real' is unknowable, but some forms are pragmatic or possess fidelity and probability, or scenes, plots, act, agency, purpose.	Narrative is a sign system separated from knowledge of the signified; narrative is rhetorical device; contextualist epistemology of historical event unfolding in the present.	Collect and contrast form of the narrative and coherence of narrative elements.
Pragmatist Pierce and Pepper; Microstoria work e.g. Ginzburg, Muir, Levi	Assertion of the reality of general terms or laws. Meaning is oriented toward the future.	Ideas are not mere abstractions; they are essences – things are what they are. Names are intended to show the nature of things. 'Any sort of fact is easily real for a contextualist' (Pepper, 1942: 143).	History session by the actors. Learning from the past in view of future action.

(contd.)

Table 1.2 (contd.)

Narratology	Ontology	Epistemology	Methodology
Social constructionist Burger and Luckmann Geertz Blumer/Mead Denzin Weick Gergen(s)	Individual and socially constructed realities.	Narrative is subjective account reified as objective knowledge. Narratives are acts of sensemaking.	Explore relative differences in narrative social construction.
Poststructuralist Derrida DeMan Culler Fairclough Foucault (archaeology) White and Epston	There is no outside to inside text duality or originary narrative.	Narratives are intertextual to knowledge of other narratives; narratives are ideological with political consequences.	Deconstructive reading of narratives.
Critical theorist Marx Marcuse Horkheimer Adorno Debord in situationist movement	Historical materialism (even dialectic teleology) shaped by class, ethnicity, gender and socioeconomic values.	Grand narratives dominate local knowledge. But there can be local resistance to grand knowledge narratives.	Hegemonic reading of narratives; ideology readings of narratives.
Postmodernist Best and Kellner (on Debord) Baudrillard Lyotard Jameson Deleuze and Guattari	Virtual and cultural hyperreal, skeptic critiques of late capitalism, to affirmation of spiritual world.	Knowledge and power are narratively fragmented; to affirmative knowledge living cosmos.	Polyphonic and juxtaposed readings and writing of a chorus of narratives.

theme analysis, but opens up the hierarchy of classification to see what gets left out. This is my contribution. Antenarrative highlights the story-telling moves and flows beyond the limits of theme analysis. Antenarra-tive analysis combined with theme analysis reconnects to stories of time, place, plurality and connectivity. In this way antenarrative is a way to resituate the duality between narrative and story (see Culler, 1980: 169–87). It allows the excess and in-between of theme analysis to move out of the margins. Beyond the tidy logic of theme taxonomy is the messy plenitude of storytelling. This is a narrating space where the economy runs on stories not analysis. Antenarrative reconnects theme analysis to fragmen-tation, the becoming and the undoing of self-deconstruction.

Why study narrative and antenarrative?

Narratologies are boundless and wonderfully varying. Manning and Cullum-Swan (1996) provide a useful review as do Czarniawska (1997), and Fairhurst and Putnam (1999) for the interested reader. Such review is beyond the scope of our eight narrative analysis chapters. But reading these and other reviews suggests to me that this is a contested domain. 'Narratology is the theory and systematic study of narrative' (Currie, 1998: 1), but it is also the clash of many disciplines. My short list of narra-tologies ranges from realist to structuralist, social constructionist, post-structuralist, critical theorist and postmodernist (see Table 1.2). The scientific study of narrative structure is in film, history, literature, adver-tising, comics, and organization and family life.

For two decades poststructuralists and some postmodernists and critical theorists have deployed *deconstruction* to declare the death of several other narratology sciences, a move that realist, structuralist and social construc-tionist narratologies did not notice or elected to ignore. Social construction, for example, is alleged to exclude politics, economics, ecology and ideo-logy in its narrative organization studies and narrative organization change projects.

In sum, the main change in narrative sciences has been to pay closer attention to alternatives to narrative analysis. Organization study, in my view, has rarely stepped outside the single-voiced, third-person narrative analysis to gaze at the conditions of antenarrative. My goal is to embrace narrative analysis alternatives that would tell organization stories differently, that would resituate narrative analysis to rebalance the hier-archical domination of narrative over story. It is not to abandon narrative analysis, but to look at how to analyse fragmented and almost living stories (TwoTrees, 1997), which are to me the currency of organizational communication.

1

Deconstruction analysis

Deconstruction is antenarrative in action. Every story excludes. Every story legitimates a centred point of view, a worldview, or an ideology among alternatives. No story is ideologically neutral; story floats in the chaotic soup of bits and pieces of story fragments. Story is never alone; it lives and breathes its meaning in a web of other stories. And, every story since it is embedded in changing meaning contexts of multiple stories and collective story making, 'self-deconstructs' with each telling. Deconstruction is both phenomenon and analysis. It is phenomenon because 'story deconstruction' is all the constructing and reconstructing processes happening all around us. It is analysis, as I have come to read it. I will speak of two levels: the level of action and the analytic level.

I will follow Derrida in asserting that the stories are self-deconstructing on their own. But I differ because I do posit several analytical steps. These are steps I will describe as 'story deconstruction' analysis. Of course, my deconstruction is already unravelling and can be deconstructed, having the traces of its own self-deconstruction. Here I will briefly define deconstruction, specify several analytic steps and develop examples.

What is deconstruction?

Deconstructionists point out the instability, complex movements, processes of change, and the play of differences and heterogeneity that make stability, unity, structure, function and coherence one-sided readings. Structure, form and coherence are stability metaphors readers impose upon narrative to render them as object-like. Deconstructionists argue that each reading is an active disturbance and a metaphor-projection by a reader that constructs the narrative-object. We do not need to deconstruct management and organization stories since, however authoritatively they are told and however logically they are narrated, they are already deconstructing and reconstructing without the help of an analyst. Indeed, just our reading and retelling of a management story is a deconstructive action.

There are excellent studies and reviews of the relation of deconstruction to critical theory and postmodern organization studies. For example, critical theorists such as Alvesson and Willmott (1996) seek to marry deconstruction to the critical theory revival of Marxist critiques of ideology.

Without searches for ideology, critical theorists were concerned that deconstruction became just another formalism, anti-historical, politically conservative, and like the other narratologies, lacking a social change project. Alvesson and Deetz (1996) called for organization studies to look at critical theory and postmodern theory as complementary, stronger together than apart. See Kilduff's (1993) deconstruction analysis of March and Simon's classic text *Organizations* and Martin's (1990) deconstruction of an executive's narrative of a manager's pregnancy.

Should we define deconstruction?

'Deconstruction,' argues Mark Currie in his book on *Postmodern Narrative*, 'can be used as an umbrella term under which many of the most important changes in narratology can be described, especially those which depart from the very scientific analysis by which it operated before post-structuralist critiques impacted on literary studies' (1998: 3). Currie's project is to merge structuralist and poststructuralist narratology, and thus he coins the term 'socio-narratology'.

Stories are not ideology-neutral, not even those formal science narratives that stress realism, verifiability and replication. Social, economic and political values intrude upon narratives. Narratives in organization studies and in the *Wall Street Journal* are ideological, and legitimate the empire building of leaders, nations and organizations. In the alternative presses and the world wide web, however, the boycotts of critical and postmodern activists tell other stories. Since deconstruction can and does expose ideological tracks behind a status quo story line, there is ample resistance.

Definitions of deconstructions are avoided. One I like is by Joanne Martin. She defines deconstruction:

> as an analytic strategy that exposes in a systematic way multiple ways a text can be interpreted. Deconstruction is able to reveal ideological assumptions in a way that is particularly sensitive to the suppressed interests of members of disempowered, marginalized groups. (1990: 340)

For me, deconstruction is a postructuralist epistemology, not a formula-method with steps and procedures. Defining deconstruction may be contrary to the spirit of Derrida's writing. Yet, deconstruction often does involve ways of reading that decentre or otherwise unmask narratives that posit authoritative centres. 'According to Derrida, all Western thought is based on the idea of a center – an origin, a Truth, and Ideal Form, a fixed Point, an Immovable Mover, an Essence, a God, a Presence, which is usually capitalized, and guarantees all meaning' (Powell, 1997: 21). But, caution is in order. If we just replace one centre with our own authoritative centre, we have fallen into our own trap. The point then is not to replace one centre with another, but to show how each centre is in a constant state of change and disintegration. The more a narrative works to control a centre, even one with a grain of truth, the more the narrative spirals out of control.

Misinterpretations of deconstruction

Jacques Derrida (1999: 65–83) gave an interview published by Kearney and Dooley (1999) that I think resolves four basic misunderstandings:

1. **Is deconstruction a method?** Derrida contends that deconstruction is not a philosophy or a method, nor is it a periodizing phase or a moment (1999: 65). Rather, deconstruction happens. It is like the entropy that is all around us. Within organization studies, to paraphrase Derrida (1999: 72), there is a history of concepts that are being transformed, deconstructed, criticized and improved. The same is true of organizations: the concepts, theories, paradigms and narratives are being deconstructed. Transformations, deconstruction and reformation are part of the ongoing organizing process. Nevertheless, I think there are ways to trace the influence of deconstruction as Table 1.1 presents. This has to do with paying attention to the heterogeneous, multiplicity of textual and intertextual processes from duality to resituation. But, I freely admit these are my own reconstructions of Derrida. Yet, as Derrida remarks 'the strategy of deconstruction is: I interpret a way to understand micro-power and 'what powers may be in such and such a context' (1999: 74). Deconstruction as a strategy, not a method, traces the micro-power of textual process, exposing centralizing and unravelling aspects, making less visible aspects more apparent.

2. **Does deconstruction equal destruction?** Derrida (1999) contends that deconstruction is not 'negative' it is something that is happening, and it does not imply that construction is not also happening. 'I have always insisted deconstruction is not destruction, is not annihilation, is not negative' (Derrida, 1999: 77). And he continues, 'as soon as you realize that deconstruction is not something negative, you cannot simply oppose it to reconstruction. How could you reconstruct anything without deconstruction?' (1999: 77).

3. **Is deconstruction extreme relativism?** There are some critics who contend that there must be only one truth and that admitting that there is not means all truths are equal or relative. What such an argument ignores are the grounded and situated aspects of discursive networks among stakeholders. As Derrida responds:

> What is relativism? Are you a relativist simply because you say, for instance, that the other is the other, and that every other is other than the other? If I want to pay attention to the singularity of the other, the singularity of the situation, the singularity of language, is that relativism? ... No, relativism is a doctrine which has its own history in which there are only points of view with no absolute necessity, or no references to absolutes. That is the opposite to what I have to say .... I have never said such a thing. Neither have I ever used the word relativism. (1999: 78)

Table 1.1   *Story deconstruction guidelines* (adapted from Boje and Dennehy, 1993)

Story deconstruction

1. *Duality search.* Make a list of any bipolar terms, any dichotomies that are used in the story. Include the term even if only one side is mentioned. For example, in male-centred and/or male-dominated organization stories, men are central and women are marginal others. One term mentioned implies its partner.

2. *Reinterpret the hierarchy.* A story is one interpretation or hierarchy of an event from one point of view. It usually has some form of hierarchical thinking in place. Explore and reinterpret the hierarchy (e.g. in duality terms how one dominates the other) so you can understand its grip.

3. *Rebel voices.* Deny the authority of the one voice. Narrative centres marginalize or exclude. To maintain a centre takes enormous energy. What voices are not being expressed in this story? Which voices are subordinate or hierarchical to other voices (e.g. Who speaks for the trees?)?

4. *Other side of the story.* Stories always have two or more sides. What is the other side of the story (usually marginalized, under-represented, or even silent)? Reverse the story, by putting the bottom on top, the marginal in control, or the back stage up front. For example, reverse the male-centre, by holding a spotlight on its excesses until it becomes a female centre in telling the other side; the point is not to replace one centre with another, but to show how each centre is in a constant state of change and disintegration.

5. *Deny the plot.* Stories have plots, scripts, scenarios, recipes and morals. Turn these around (move from romantic to tragic or comedic to ironic).

6. *Find the exception.* Stories contain rules, scripts, recipes and prescriptions. State each exception in a way that makes it extreme or absurd. Sometimes you have to break the rules to see the logic being scripted in the story.

7. *Trace what is between the lines.* Trace what is not said. Trace what is the writing on the wall. Fill in the blanks. Storytellers frequently use 'you know that part of the story.' Trace what you are filling in. With what alternate way could you fill it in (e.g. trace to the context, the back stage, the between, the intertext)?

8. *Resituate.* The point of doing 1 to 7 is to find a new perspective, one that resituates the story beyond its dualisms, excluded voices or singular viewpoint. The idea is to reauthor the story so that the hierarchy is resituated and a new balance of views is attained. Restory to remove the dualities and margins. In a resituated story there are no more centres. Restory to script new actions.

It is not that 'one can say anything' that matters; it is that there are socially situated limits and 'what one can assert'. There is a juridical and political limit on extreme relativity. The charge of relativism begs the question: can there be an ethic in postmodernism and poststructuralism? Bauman (1993) asserts there is a postmodern ethics. As Derrida puts it 'I take into account differences, but I am no relativist' (1999: 79).

4. **Is there an outside to text?** Derrida is often critiqued for saying there is nothing outside of the text, a move which would deny that there are birds, trees and the Holocaust. But, what did he say? 'Il n'y a pas dehors-texte' is Derrida's most misinterpreted slogan, and according to

Currie 'does not mean there is nothing outside the text as most commentators have taken it. It is closer to "There is no outside-text"' (1998: 45). The confusion is that Derrida indicates that outside the text are other texts, but also material conditions of textual production, and text traced into material conditions (i.e. factories, schools, bombs, genocide and war). Derrida clarifies that 'what I call the "text" is not distinct from action or opposed to action' (1999: 65). A text is not the pages of a book, it is a much broader concept that includes the politics and ethics of action. 'The distinction between truth and reality is absolutely elementary, as is the distinction between truth and veracity; that is, to say something is true does not mean that you say something is real' (1999: 77).

With apologies to Derrida, I will outline eight analytic moves to decentre and deconstruct stories (see Table 1.1).

The eighth move

Critics of deconstruction call my first seven tactics in Table 1.1 mere destruction, but I think that is because they do not see or maybe refuse to see the end game, the eighth move, as deconstruction is controversial. Structuralists have raised counter-charges about the political right politics of deconstructionist, Paul de Man, in a witchhunt for his wartime journalism with the Nazi propaganda machine. 'The wartime journalism – mostly inoffensive reviews for a collaborationist newspaper in Belgium – was widely viewed as confirmation of the latent fascism in deconstructive narratology' (Currie, 1998: 7). There has been a backlash from this controversy about deconstruction and ideology in *Organization Science* (Boje, 2000a; Weiss, 2000). Others have said I err because I make deconstruction too easy and too accessible. A few students have told me that deconstruction is negative thinking and does not lead to solutions or to change of any kind. I do not apologize for making it accessible and I contend deconstruction can result in change and solutions. Many critics, I believe, do not make the eighth move. The eighth move, as presented in Table 1.1, is to *resituate* the dualities, voices and traces, and its hierarchy into a new rendering of a story. In this restorying, there is the possibility of new action, of a way out of hierarchy and domination. Of course at the action level, resituation is happening anyway, to analyse it is to note its unfolding.

Narrative constructs centres that marginalize or exclude. For example, in a bureaucracy, men are often given the central roles and become the spokesmen for the organization, while women's voices are silent, not authorized to speak for the corporation (Clair, 1998). If we reverse the male-centre, by holding a spotlight on its excesses until it becomes a female centre, this may be fair, just and reasonable, but it would fall short of what we seek in deconstruction. That is, a resituation of the narrative so that there are no more centres, male or female. We can make the same case about race, ethnic and managerial control narratives that are centred on one element at the exclusion of others. To maintain a centre takes enormous energy. And since no narrative is an island, but in a dynamic context of a plurality of other narratives, the centred position self-deconstructs without any pushing, shoving or editing on our part. The epistemology of deconstruction is one of dynamic intertextuality, of constant change and self-deconstruction.

Eight deconstructive moves

Duality search

I assume stories are told in ways that seek centres and proliferate many binary opposites: male/female, organization/environment, white/black, heterosexual/homosexual, quantitative/qualitative, management/worker, permanent/temporary, old/young, etc. The point of reading a story for its dualizing terms is to see the play of differences, how each term seeks to represent many different terms. In male/female, for example, both 'male' and 'female' are cover terms representing many variations. There are macho males and gentle males, gay and straight males, just as there are variations of femininity. Derrida writes of reading to see how the text (or story) self-deconstructs, how the author of a story has reversed his/her own (dualized) hierarchy of binary terms, privileging the marginal over the dominant. For example, privileging a male story over a female story, or a particular masculinity or femininity over others. Like structuralism and formalism, deconstruction is sensitive to binary oppositions in narrating, but looks for the unstable qualities of binaries, not their stabilizing structural footprints. A deconstructive reading of narrative traces the hierarchy in the opposition between a dominating and a marginalized or subordinated binary term. Review the narrative to isolate the most problematic dualities where one term is central or privileged while the 'other' is marginal, repressed or excluded. When just one term is mentioned, record the silence of its opposite. It is reading 'between the lines' of the text, an implied term conspicuous by its absence (Boje and Dennehy, 1993). Look at the fictions. Look at the haves and have-nots. Look for the propaganda. Where is the text selling you a central vision, utopian dream, progress-myth, essentialist concept or transcendent principle? Like now, I am selling you that narratives have centres, and that they hide peripheries. Mills and Simmons (1994) refer to this as a search for assumptions, silences, exclusions, deletions, asides and illustrations that contain hierarchies. If you only read the propaganda, you can be seduced into assuming that white is black, a dictator is a democrat, and chauvinists are feminists. Finding the dualities means lifting the veil of propaganda to let the 'constructions' deconstruct, and doing so without laying tracks for an alternative propaganda.

Reinterpret the hierarchy

The hierarchy lives in the value systems you are trying to analyse. It can be a most violent hierarchy in which the centred term becomes the Real and the Good while the oppressed or excluded becomes the Unreal and the Bad, something to be burned at the stake. Or it can be more hidden and taken-for-granted, a subtle hegemony that goes unnoticed, moving behind the scenes to tilt other binaries this way or that. In much of organization theory (OT) the binaries are 'managerialist' in their ideology: 'male-centred', with 'white' and 'Anglo' assumptions about the manager's perspectives being more right or having more 'real' agency or being more the way of free market economies. One way to reinterpret the hierarchy is reversal. 'For example, a reversal of binary opposition might be overthrowing patriarchy for matriarchy' (Clair, 1998: 110). As Clair observes, this just replaces one hierarchy with its reversal. Yet, the reversal can open up the analysis and let us think differently. What if we reverse manager/work hierarchy and let workers control or exercise democratic governance? In the reversal, the workers cannot so easily be framed as bad, lazy, in need of motivation and too uneducated to manage themselves. You see how I am sneaking in my own ideology of workers' democracy in my reversal. In Marxist narratives, which I do seem to prefer, the reversal happens, the workers' viewpoint has privilege over the capitalists and their manager-agents. In the reversal, capitalists are blood-sucking vampires squeezing the last ounce of blood out of labour.

Derrida says Western thought forms these binary opposites, putting them into hierarchies. It is not always easy to find hierarchy because a narrative may pretend to narrate the *only* 'true' reality. A democratic or ecologist narrative (obviously better than a managerialist, I am being ironic, or am I?), may present ways of being democratic that are hierarchic and elitist. One term may be vocal while the other is absent, silent or a supplement to the primary term. Labour can be in the discourse used, a 'supplement' to management, and vice versa.

In French, *supplement* has a double meaning: to add on to a thing already complete in itself, or to complete the thing by adding on to it. In managerialism, labour is corrupting, perverse, lazy and undependable, an expensive item that needs to be controlled and abandoned. Sometimes the marginal term is not in the text at all, it is in the implied, but missing half of duality. There is hierarchy in this string of implied binaries. 'Organizations would be great places if it were not for employees,' says the managerialist. 'Organizations would be great places if not for managers,' says the Marxist. The deconstructive proof is to show how a narrative (including this one) is able to accomplish the little propaganda steps that get you to buy into what it is selling you, its perspective above all others. Where do you begin hierarchy analysis? Trace where the rhetoric does not live up to its own expectations or is even the opposite of what it says it does. Show how the narrative constructs a hierarchy by privileging one term over the other. The left term dominates the right in many business contexts:

Central :/: Marginal
Organization :/: Environment
Management :/: Labour
Capital :/: Labour
Male :/: Female
Faculty :/: Student
US :/: Third World
Narrative :/: Story

Rebel voices

There are voices that do not get included in a given telling of a story. My friend Robert Gephart Jr., for example, is concerned with ecology. He will hear a story about business and the natural environment, and ask 'who speaks for the trees?'. Perhaps it is the community that is left out of a story about commissioners deciding where to locate a new toxic waste disposal site; or, an organization change story, where the voice of the people being changed is not a part of the story. In these stories there is good opportunity to write up a counter-narrative that tells the story with the 'rebel voice'. Putting this rebel story side by side with the 'dominant' original story puts both in a new context of meaning. For example, Joanne Martin's (1990) article deconstructs and reconstructs a story told by a large multinational corporate president from a feminist perspective. She examines what the story says, what it does not say, and what might have said. This is the story told by the CEO to a university conference audience:

> We have a young woman who is extraordinarily important to the launching of a major new (product). We will be talking about it next Tuesday in its first world wide introduction. She has arranged to have her Caesarean yesterday in order to be prepared for this event, so you – We have insisted that she stay home and this is going to be televised in a closed circuit television, so we're having this done by TV for her, and she is staying home three months and we are finding ways of filling in to create this void for us because we think it's an important thing for her to do. (1990: 339)

The story begins 'We have a young woman ...' rather than 'A young woman works for us' (1990: 344). 'Having,' argues Martin 'suggests that the company has access to the whole of the woman – her health and her homelife – as well as her work' (1990: 345). The employment contract gives employers control over work behaviour, but leaves homelife, and medical treatment and their timing choices to the employee. The story implies that the timing and choice of the Caesarean operation 'she arranged' had to do with the corporation 'being prepared for' and 'the launching of a major new (product)' and 'its world wide introduction'. 'We have insisted that she stay home' indicates that the corporation ('we') 'took responsibility for making decisions that are usually the responsibility of a doctor and a patient – not an employer' (1990: 345). The company 'we're having this done by TV for her' initiated the closed circuit TV installed in the employee's bedroom. Martin contends that the employee has lost control over the private decisions about what goes on in her bedroom. The corporation, she argues, may be invading her privacy or she may have welcomed the TV's installation. The gaps in the story speak powerfully of hierarchy.

The voice of corporate control dominates this story and the word choices may indicate levels of discomfort and tension at the interpenetration of work and home contexts. The discursive utterances of the CEO storyteller announce the problematic juxtaposition of work and homelife. There is instability in the story lines in which perhaps the teller's subconscious begins to speak in Freudian slips. Martin rewrites the story with a rebel voice, changing the female character to a man. Since men do not have Cesarean surgery, she reconstructs the story line with a male surgery.

> We have a young man who is extraordinarily important to the launching of a major new (product). We will be talking about it next Tuesday in its first world wide introduction. He has arranged [sic] to have his coronary bypass operation yesterday in order to be prepared for this event, so you – We have insisted that he stay home and this is going to be televised in a closed circuit television, so we're having this done by TV for him, and he is staying home three months and we are finding ways of filling in to create this void for us because we think it's an important thing for him to do. (1990: 346)

Another rebel voice is revealed – the unborn child. In the bypass, only the man's life is in jeopardy by changing the timing of the operation. 'The Cesarean story suggests that the mother may have jeopardized her child, or at least altered the timing of its birth to fit the schedule of a product introduction' (Martin, 1990: 347).

Other side of the story

Reversing the hierarchy replaces one centre with another. Yet, it is a useful way to trace differences. Once you can state the hierarchic relationship between the two terms, you can describe the play of differences of variants within each term. This assumes there are subtle and complex variations in each term of the duality, e.g. managers are also employees, professors are also managers, and students are also the eyes of the administration. Similarly, a bureaucracy can take many forms: corrupt, red tape, protector of the weak, predictable processes, due process, restraint of abusive power. Reversing means to look at the ways in which the other term is sometimes and in some ways the more dominant term. For example, re-engineering may say it 'bashes' and 'smashes' Adam Smith's division of labour or Max Weber's bureaucracy, but re-engineering also creates bureaucracy, division of labour, cyber-mechanical processes, and here and there, destroys the flexibility that is its claim to fame.

Subvert the original hierarchy between the central and marginal term of the duality by listing the variations and subtle differences and manifestations of each term. For example, show how the dominant term is a special case of the marginal term, and vice versa. Boje and Dennehy (1993) call it 'rebel voices': giving voice to the marginal perspectives. This leads you to see reversals in the dominant hierarchy. You can usually show how the author's centrist narrative deconstructs itself. The author may provide clues and traces of the hierarchy and its own reversals. It is like seeing the trace of a plane in the cloud-prints, but not seeing a plane. For example, if you look at phallologocentric (male organ + logic) management texts, many of the preferred qualities of a leader such as being social, team-oriented, nurturing, and sensitive as a communicator are ideal qualities generally associated with the female. Isolating ideals is the point of this phase of the analysis. In the reversal, female begins to dominate male, as the implied supplement. At this stage, we have only replaced one dominant relationship with its opposite. This can mean substituting a feminist, ethnic, non-White, non-European or non-managerialist assumption set for the hierarchies in the text. There is more to do.

Deny the plot
Stories have plots, scripts, scenarios, recipes and morals. Yet, in antenarrative the plots are not agreed upon, there is dissensus over whose plot gets precedence (see Chapter 7). Plots also convey a theory of causality, who or what caused an event, and what events are inter-connected (see Chapter 6). Plots known since Plato are romantic, tragic, comedic and ironic. Many of the narratives I read in management and organization textbooks have a romantic plot that does not get denied. The CEO is always the hero, the Fortune 500 company is always engaged in 'progress' to provide secure jobs and clean up the environment. Yet, in the alternative press, there are stories about these same CEOs and corporations that are not so romantic. In fact, you can find quite tragic stories about many (not all) that are about labour and environmental tragedy. And in Doonsebury and other cartoon-stories you sometimes find comedy and irony. The plot of the story is also a script for how to behave, a scenario of what follows what, and often, the story ends with a self-evident moral claim. Turn these plots, scripts, scenarios, recipes and morals around to highlight the centring devices. This can be accomplished by tracing the story plot to different plots in other stories. Tracing a story into its inter-story context (into the Tamara of many prenarrated stories and antenarratives) also invites a political reading of the text in intertextual relation to other texts. How does the story reference a context of other antenarratives, self-destructing one meaning in a web or network of stories of other meanings (see Chapter 4)?

Find the exception
What is the exception that breaks the rule that does not fit the storied recipe or moral and somehow escapes the strictures of the principle? The fun thing about a rule is that there are always exceptions. These exceptions

can be located in the context of the storied situation, that is, in the intertextual arena of other stories (see Chapter 5). There are other stories about the rule being centred and showcased, and these can be stories where the rule does not hold. Since rules and what they purport to 'fix' are always in flux and change, the exceptions are emerging all the time. State the rule in a way that makes it seem extreme or absurd, or just point out some of the ways it is self-deconstructing with changes in context. A rule such as 'you can't change that', or 'there's nothing you can do about it, [or] [M]en are just that way' can be challenged (Clair, 1998: 81) because rules are political constructions that help to reify hierarchy (Mumby, 1987). Clair (1998) argues that such rules help to silence sexual harassment stories, keeping them part of the private domain 'we don't talk about that' or used to deny personal experience in favour of narratives that follow the bureaucratic rules. For example in the 'bureaucratization of sexual harassment' the rules are it is not 'harassment' unless you 'say no', 'keep a record', of each occurrence, and 'report it' to the proper channels. And what happens when you follow the rules, say in universities? 'Oddly enough, "report it" seems to be the end of the story for most universities. The exchange has been completed' (Clair, 1998: 117). The irony is all three rules act to 'bureaucratize, commodify, and privatize sexual harassment'. If we deny the rules, we expose some interesting stereotypes. For example, 'the requirement of documentation perpetuates the stereotype that women lack credibility; that sexual harassment without witnesses, times, dates, and so on also lacks credibility; and that written codes (i.e., documentation) create a false reality that action is being taken' (Clair, 1998: 119).

State what is between the lines
Trace what is not said. Read between the story lines. Trace what is the writing on the wall and where people resist by being silent. Fill in the blanks as you trace. Storytellers frequently use 'you know that part of the story.' What are you filling in as you read 'you know' the story? With what alternate ways could you fill it in (e.g. get at the context, the back stage, the between)? It is a question of systematically tracing how the story encourages you to borrow from a heritage of other stories. Some of the stories are your own life experiences. Others are stories the story you read refers back to. Each story inscribes another story. Each story is related intertextually to another story (see Chapter 5). A very brief story, told to those in the know, can key the story co-creators (tellers and co-tellers, and co-listeners) to recall a more extensive story line. When we tell a story to people who know the longer version, we sometimes skip the details and speak a few coded lines. But these abbreviated lines refer to lines that are not said; ones we are expected to imagine. They are traces of lines between the lines of the story. Derrida puts it this way in *Grammatology*:

> This trace is the opening of the first exteriority in general, the enigmatic relationship of the living to its other and of an inside to an outside: spacing. The outside, 'spatial' and 'objective' exteriority which we believe we know as the

most familiar thing in the world, as familiarity itself, would not appear with
out the grammê, without différance as temporalization, without the nonpres-
ence of the other inscribed within the meaning of the present, without the
relation to death as the concrete structure of the living present .... The
presence-absence of the trace .... (1976: 41–3)

Hegemony (passive, taken-for-granted and spontaneous assent) and coercion (force) are ways to organize silence, ways for dominant groups to
control others: 'silencing groups of people may take on a multitude of
forms ... silence may be achieved through coercion or through hegemony'
(Clair, 1998: 67). A noisy CEO can silence everyone else; a meeting set up
with no time for questions is a way to silence. But being silent is also a
way, maybe the only way, to express resistance. Reading the silence
between the lines is a way to deconstruct the forces that oppress.

Resituate
The first seven steps allow us to get to this point. The task of resituation
is to remove the domination of the hierarchy of the duality in the story. It
is time to renarrate the narrative. Show how the narrative can become or
sometimes is a free play of the binary opposites beyond hierarchy. At the
very least, two readings of the binary (one reversed) can be suspended in
the undecidability of double logic. When there is no central configuration
the text is non-hierarchical; it is double meaning. The problem is how to
do this without replacing one centre for another centre (one hierarchy for
another). It does little good to replace a male hierarchy with a female one
or one racist hierarchy for another one. What is it like to behave in a new
praxis, a new pattern of behaviours without hierarchy? Boje and Dennehy
(1993) call this writing a new plot or restorying beyond the dominant
hierarchies. The resituation of the text is what Mills and Simmons (1994)
refer to as 're-Writing the Text to create new 'praxis'. Praxis means experi-
menting and testing out new actions and relationships. What could it
look like? The new narrative you create can become the subject of another
deconstruction, another exploration of binary, hierarchy, reversal and
resituation.

Barbara Czarniawska (1999) commenting about the art of Maurits
Cornelis Escher (1898–1972) pointed out that much of management and
organization theory is focused above the water line seeing only the black
swans, while we deconstructionists focus below the water line seeing the
fish. The idea of deconstruction is to see both images, to do a double
visioning. Figure 1.1 captures what I mean by deconstruction. It is looking beneath the surface of the story.

Example: deconstructing the capital/labour duality

Jacques Derrida has looked at Marxism. In his address, the 'Specters of
Marx', Derrida (1994) plays with the philosophical term, 'ontology', by
introducing the term 'hauntology'. Ontology looks at 'Being in the world',

Source: M.C. Escher works, Cordon Art, Baarn, the Netherlands.

Figure 1.1   *Escher's black swans and fish*

while hauntology looks at the space between being and non-being, the place of ghosts and spectres. In approaching Marx, Derrida is able to move beyond the duality of capital/labour to look in-between at the hauntology of Marxism.

In Marx's *Communist Manifesto* (1848), Marx uses the word 'specter'. 'A specter is haunting Europe, the specter of Communism.' The powers of Europe seek to conjure away or exorcise this spectre. After the Berlin Wall fell, many assumed that indeed Marxism was dead and that monopoly capitalism was triumphant. But, with labour process theory and Neo-Marxism, the ghost of Marxism keeps haunting capitalism. Braverman (1974) acknowledges a common duality that we unravel with several of the approaches in Table 1.1.

Find the dualities
Braverman says that capital and labour constitute a giant duality (1974: 377). Braverman views managers as agents who while sharing in

'subjugation and oppression' that characterize the lives of workers (1974: 418), occupy positions of comparative privilege. As agents of capital, managers are hired to pump surplus value out of labour. Managers control the labour process to maximize capitalist profit and accumulation rather than increasing the self-determination, skill and wage condition of workers. The duality here is capital/labour.

Articulate the hierarchy
Capital dominates labour, or as Braverman puts it: 'Capital is labour' (1974:). This means that labour produces the surplus value (over wage value) that becomes profit. Explore the hierarchy: capital appropriates labour (knowledge of labour becomes systemic knowledge) in its acts of greedy accumulation of more and more capital as labour is squeezed into poverty and dependency. Labour becomes more and more marginal as it is displaced by automation, de-skilled and substituted for cheaper labour (agricultural labour and females employed at lower wages). This is where the labour process theory (the question I asked of you) gets articulated concisely:

- Capital dominates labour by **mechanization and automation** to keep the number of workers in a given industry to a minimum (1974: 381). The mechanization of jobs produces surplus populations (of unemployed, under-employed or partially employed adults) which drives the pay of labour down (1974: 382–3).
- Capital, says Marx 'thrusts itself frantically into old branches of production … transformation of a part of the laboring population into unemployed or half-employed hands' (Marx as cited in Braverman, 1974: 383). *'The purpose of machinery is not to increase but to decrease the number of workers attached to it'* (1974: 384).
- **Race** comes into play as the Black, Spanish and Asian countries and populations become reservoirs of the lowest paid labour (1974: 384–5).
- **Gender** comes into play as women are funnelled into much lower paying jobs to supplement the race-reservoir of labour.
- **The industrial reserve army** has three parts:

    1. the **floating** employees who move from job to job;
    2. the **latent** workers found in agricultural areas (e.g. Nike's recruitment in China, Vietnam and Indonesia) and
    3. the **stagnant** surplus of workers who no longer can find work and get to live as paupers (1974: 386–7). The first and second are the 'concealed proportion of the population who do not show up in the unemployment statistic. Males, particularly Black males in the US have been moved, more and more into the stagnant sector, while lower-paid women and exported jobs increase' (1974: 391–3).

- As wealth increases, the industrial reserve army also increases as does the torment and misery of labour (1974: 396). *This is the* **absolute general law of capitalist accumulation** (1974: 388–9). As capital accumulates, so does misery.
- With the **technical division of labour and hierarchical control**, the labour process can be 'rationalized' (1974: 408).
- The **service sector** of lower and lower paid jobs expands in proportion to the industrial reserve army.
- Finally, the **clerical and middle management** ranks are being subjected now to these same trends.
- In sum, this is the labour process theory, the movement of mass numbers of higher paid and highly skilled males into the industrial reserve army, while the rulers of industry take out larger and larger pay and stock options for themselves. With more information technology the ranks and pay of middle management continue to decline.

Reverse the duality
Braverman deconstructs his own duality. He notes that 'Labour is Capital' (1974: 377). Capital depends upon labour to extract its capital surplus. Not only workers, but managers (especially middle ones) are subjugated and oppressed. Another reversal: the individual entrepreneur, says Max Weber, is indeed a capitalist. The capitalist in building a business chooses between adopting a feudal and a bureaucratic structure. Capital in the dysfunctional side of bureaucracy pays labour subsistence wages, substitutes de-skilled labour for skilled labour puts people in a hierarchy of specialized ranks and functions – and overtime moves wages below the poverty line. Marx wrote about the need to exorcise Marxism from capitalism. This could be our Western inability to look at under-employment, homelessness, child labour, racism, de-skilling, sexism, environmental deterioration as a cost of business that is shunted onto tax payers. The ghost of Marxism goes beyond the totalitarian repression that fell (we hope) with the Berlin Wall. Derrida sees deconstruction as a more radical form of Marxism. To reverse the duality would make labour more important than capital. There are systems of enterprise, such as coops and worker-owned firms where labour is capital. There are also firms such as Body Shop, Ben and Jerry's, Toms of Maine, etc. that put social and environmental responsibility ahead of CEO greed.

Resituate the duality
In resituation we look at the larger context in which capital and labour are in interplay in the global economy. There are examples of greed and non-greed in business formation. Labour can and does resist the greed form of capitalism. Capital is dependent on labour and therefore labour can be radical and democratic in its reversal of human and ecological destruction (Alvesion and Willmott, 1996). A resituation looks at how managers are

manipulated and encouraged to suspend their personal values and ethics while pursuing surplus value maximizing strategies.

Managers, for example, are seduced and controlled by elaborate bonus, profit sharing and stock schemes to keep extracting surplus value from labour. Both managers and workers are caught up in a panopoly of disciplinary and panoptic mechanisms (Foucault, 1979). Senior managers elevate the profit maximizing goal above all else (do the bidding of capital to the detriment of the workforce). But, is managerial work wholly structured by capital? The manager speaks a discourse about profit-only, but also engages in family and community discourse. Labour protests and submits, rebels or is integrated into this system (Braverman, 1974: 378) which puts the system ahead of the individuals.

To move beyond the duality is to see that labour can have interest in corporate success and that management can experience a multiplicity of selfhoods, only one of which is being capital's surplus maximizing agent. This was the concern of Mary Parker Follett (1941), to get workers trained in the economics of the firm, its market and industry. In this way worker democracy could be possible.

Still it is no accident that managers have a privileged and distant position from workers. And it is no accident that workers are kept out of corporate governance and away from a knowledge of business context and circumstance. It is a social division of labour that allows managers to continue as dedicated agents of capital. But, in the resituation, I have argued that both worker and manager are not so unitary, as the labour process characterization has advocated. We can look more carefully at how capital disciplines managers to be its executioners and how managers resist this role.

The value of looking at labour process theory is to see how new fads (i.e. such as the team concept, TQM, reengineering, and subcontractor networking) just present the old wolf in newly fashioned sheep's clothing. The new management practices appear to be more affirming of workers, but can be seen as a new disguise for labour process and the extraction of surplus value. Teamwork, delayering and quality programmes are ways to get 'workers to identify their interests as identical to those of capital' (Lucio and Stewart, 1997). Teamwork, for example, constructs collective loyalties on internal competition within the team in ways that intensifies work (workers do the work formerly done by supervisors), stress, injury and auto-surveillance (including self-surveillance).

Derrida sees in Marx a history of Europe as a succession or museum of spectres that embody the spirit of revolution. The problem Derrida introduces, in resituating Marxism, is to look at Marx's ontology of revolution of the working poor, in the historical context of other worker revolutions (other spectres). For Marx, the use value of a product, is its real being, its ontological, 'rock bottom reality' (Powell, 1995). As a product is sold, it becomes a commodity, and is haunted by a ghost, a (no)thing – the exchange value of the product. For example, the *use value* of the 'Swoosh' in Marxist thought is a few pennies worth of fabric, while the *market value* of the Swoosh on sneakers is $80 to $180 at NikeTown. Derrida questions Marx's concept of use value. 'Is it *really* there *first*, fundamentally, **ontologically**' (Powell, 1995: 146).

The commodity and exchange values already haunt the Swoosh and the sneaker. 'Hauntology always already will have haunted ontology' (146). Derrida points out that you cannot tell the difference between use value and exchange value. Derrida, in his resituation, says that Marx could allow capitalism to speak and initiate dialogue with it. When we see labour as capital and capital as labour, we see that each haunts the other. There are variations in both and shades of difference in between. We cannot tell the one from the other. There is what Derrida calls 'undecidability'. Workers can subvert established institutions of greed by re-accumulating their skill, forming their own alliances, and sharing their own profits. What is required is to de-centre greed as the central element and thereby go beyond the binary opposite of capital and labour. The resituation takes place when neither capital or labour can purge the 'other' from its own domain. As Braverman indicates each contains the other within itself. In a duality of capital over labour, capital (and its surrogate, management) appears as 'expert', while labour is viewed as 'brainless' and eventually 'skill-less'. 'He' sits atop the hierarchy, while 'she' sits submissively below. To resituate would be to move beyond hierarchy in organizations. The so-called intelligent network, adhocracy, flexibility, de-differentiated models of organization aspire to this. There is a movement to democratize the workplace, make workers knowledgeable, as well as multi-skilled. Labour would become the expert. Those closest to the work would expertly know how to decide what to do. Instead of capitalist/labourer, each has multiple selves. Worker is both capitalist and labourer.

What my deconstructive reading of Marx does is move beyond the one story of capitalism exploiting labour. We can find marginal examples of enterprise where there are variations, even reversals to the dominant story. The greed element can be acted upon. There are microstories inside the macrostory of capitalism that deconstruct the grand narrative. Appropriately, we turn next to grand narrative analysis in Chapter 2.

2

Grand narrative analysis

In antenarrative analysis, it is important to recognize the implicit macrostory that Lyotard calls the 'Grand narrative' and to look beyond to how many 'little stories' resist. Defining grand narrative is not so easy. Lyotard employs 'metanarrative' defined as 'implying a philosophy of history ... used to legitimate knowledge' (1979/1984: xxiv), 'Grand narrative' defined as 'the hero of knowledge [who] works toward a good ethico-political end – universal peace' (1979/1984: xxiv) and 'Enlightenment narrative' defined as 'a possible unanimity between rational minds' interchangeably (1979/1984: xxiii). And Lyotard defines *postmodern* simply as 'incredulity toward metanarratives' or 'Grand narratives' (1979/1984: xxiv). I shall not dwell on definitional nuances, for I have not the space. The grand narrative is defined by Brown as a 'regime of truth' (1991: 192–3) a metanarrative that subjugates and marginalizes other dis-courses. Our task is to give you the ten examples of grand narratives in Table 2.1 and illustrate several narrative analyses. I will argue that Lyotard's work is both an insightful critique and an extremely radical and polemic approach to grand narratives that I seek to balance (i.e. some grand narratives are helpful). I will resituate grand narrative analysis by asserting that there are grand narratives that local stories resist in various ways, and that from an antenarrative view what is important is to see how grand narratives emerge, self-destruct and are resisted in webs of less dominant stories.

It is only my teasing out what is the dominant grand narrative that more local (antenarrative) stories become noticeable. In the interplay between grand and local narrative we can begin to recognize hegemony and posit the dynamics of the relationship (see Chapter 3). By hegemony, I mean how one voice is privileged in the intertextual dialogue in ways that are taken-for-granted or too subtle to be acknowledged. Here we are interested in how the grand narrative is theorized and how it attains its hegemonic power. As we will explore, each story is an intertextual net-work (see Chapters 4 and 5), a system of other texts and values referenc-ing other stories. I see the local stories not simply as interesting 'other voices', but as embedded in and sometimes resisting grand narratives. Further, in our analyses we can see how the local microstoria themselves constitute a deconstruction of the grand narrative by their resistance

Table 2.1   *Ten grand narratives of Enlightenment knowledge*

1. **Logical positivism** – Comte, Descartes, Hume respective faith in positivism,
    Cartesian dualisms, and empiricism as the path to Enlightenment. The idea
    is logical positivism can map and represent all, the whole is determinable,
    and individuals can be governed by logic and reason (instead of passions).
    It is a mechanical and 'mirror' grand narrative that replaces religion while
    claiming secular status (see Lyotard: 11–12, 46, 48, 50).

2. **Imperial politics** – For example, Napoleon's idea that to point the nation to
    'the path to progress' by direct control of higher education so as to 'produce
    the administrative and professional skills necessary for the stability of the
    State' leading the nation in the name of 'freedom' (see Lyotard: 31–2).

3. **German idealism** – For example, in the speculative model, the function
    (8 below) of the University of Berlin (founded 1807) had a different
    relation between science, nation and state than 2 above. Humboldt
    decided science (the search for true causes, e.g. 1 above) would
    orient its university research and teaching to the spiritual, moral
    and ethical (just causes) training of the nation (see Lyotard: 32, 37–8 and 52).

4. **Critical enlightenment** – As Wilber puts it 'all postmodern roads lead to
    Nietzsche' (1996: 61). Jameson argues that Lyotard's distinction between
    grand narrative and storytelling is based on 'a Nietzschean thematics
    of history' (1984: xii). Frederick Nietzsche as well as Schopenhauer were
    quite critical of 3, German idealism. However, Best and Kellner argue
    that Lyotard distorts 'a Nietzschean vitalism and dialectic of yes and no'
    into a pure affirmation philosophy of life (1991: 154, 156, 158). Best and
    Kellner originate the term 'critical enlightenment' arguing that Nietzsche
    anticipated postmodern micropolitics of desire, critiques of universalism,
    life-denying rationalism, and much else (1997: 62–3) (see Lyotard: 39, 77, 81
    and 88).

5. **Self-management** – Out of 3, German idealism, springs 'self-management'
    and the 'self-grounding of freedom' in an epic story of the subject's
    'emancipation from everything that prevents it from governing itself'
    (: 35). Lyotard draws upon Kant's 'autonomy of will' but it also parallels
    Michel Foucault's own defense of Enlightenment in *Technology of Self* and
    Care of Self books (see Lyotard: 31–6).

6. **Marxism** – Marx's *Das Kapital*. Lyotard contends 'our incredulity [to Grand
    narrative] is now such that we no longer expect salvation to rise from
    these inconsistencies [expecting less work to lower production costs and
    more work to lessen the social burden of an idle population], as did Marx'
    (1979/1984: xxiv, additions mine). Marx represents society as oppositional
    class struggle with totalizing and totalitarian effects of Stalinism (see
    Lyotard: 11, 13, 33–4 and 37).

7. **Frankfurt School** – Horkheimer, Adorno, Marcuse, Benjamin's critical theory
    followed by Habermas' defense of the unfinished projects of Enlightenment.
    Lyotard's critique of the Frankfurt School of critical theory and Jürgen
    Habermas, who claims its lineage for 'losing all of its radicality' (p. 13). Lyotard
    (p. xxv) waxes more polemic on Habermas: 'Is legitimacy to be found in
    consensus obtained through discussion, as Jürgen Habermas thinks? Such
    consensus does violence to the heterogeneity of language games. And
    invention is always born of dissension' (xxv). The other side of this story is

(contd.)

Table 2.1 (contd.)

that Habermas sees modernity as an unfinished project with many salvage oportunities (see also Lyotard: 7, 37, 60, 65 and 72).

8. **Cybernetic systems theory** – Talcott Parsons and Niklas Luhmann use structural functionalism theory to represent society as a functional and organic whole and as a self-regulating cybernetic system. Dysfunction (such as strikes, unemployment or revolution) are seen as 'internal readjustment' to increase system viability or functionality (11–12). It became popular since World War II. Lyotard points out it is 'no longer the living organism' model, but an optimistic apologetic for 'stabilization of the growth economies and societies of abundance under the aegis of a moderate welfare state' and its true goal is 'performativity' by optimizing 'the global relationship between input and output' (11) (see also Lyotard: 11–12, 46, 48–50 and 63).

9. **Post-industrial capitalism** – Daniel Bell and others (e.g. Toffler and Drucker) posit that industrial production is *passé* and it is now knowledge, science and service work that define advanced capitalist societies. Lyotard writes of producing and consuming knowledge as a commodity indispensable to multinational corporate power (4–6) and this is what other postmodern theorists call 'high or late modernism.' And it critiques alienation from computerization and miniaturization technologies of post-industrial capitalism while it ignores depleting energy and presents the progress myth (p. 7). Lyotard confuses it often with postmodern culture (See also Lyotard: 4, 7, 14 and 53 and Jameson, 1984: xiii, xx).

10. **Postmodern condition** – Lyotard's book according to Best and Kellner (1997: 154, 172–7) is itself a grand narrative using normative positions to critique others' grand narratives, and rejecting all grand narrative while posing a 'postmodern condition' grand narrative. It is a grand narrative because it argues 'since at least the end of the 1950s' advanced societies have entered 'what is known as the postmodern age' (3) (see Lyotard: 11–14 and 31).

Note: All references are to Lyotard (1979/1984).

(microstoria, and its relation to macrostory, are the subject of Chapter 3). In Chapter 2 I will give an idea of what constitutes a grand narrative and list some forms of narrative analyses that are being applied.

Grand narratives are embedded in the Enlightenment. Enlightenment grand narrative advocates, reformers and critics (1 to 10 in Table 2.1) rejected Judeo-Christian (grand) narrative content, while substituting human agency for divine fiat, progress for providence and their own poetics for religious verse (Best and Kellner, 1991; Best, 1995; Best and Kellner, 1997). Many Enlightenment grand narrative apologists were deeply religious and metaphysical, such as Comte who initiated the priesthood of positivism and pursued knowledge 'forbidden by priests and tyrants' (Lyotard, 1979: 31). Enlightenment grand narratives attempted to supplant Judeo-Christian narratives. And it seems to me each grand narrativist argues that more traditional narratives such as logical positivism, imperial politics and German idealism of nation states have given way to more contemporary postindustrial capitalism and this to the postmodern condition grand narrative. But is this so? Does the new one break up the older ones? Or is this just a way to posit one more in a long succession of grand narratives? Answers to these questions direct our analysis.

A less radical approach to grand narrative

I am more inclined to agree with Best and Kellner (1991, 1997) that Lyotard dualizes, and grand narratives can be resituated to have both strengths and limitations. We need not reject and demonize each and every one. Grand narratives of legitimation are not as obsolete as Lyotard asserts (Lyotard, 1979/1984: xxiv). There are more of them and they do not seem to fade away to be replaced by a 'postmodern Condition'. I think it makes analytic sense to look at modern and postmodern theorists who have many nuanced analyses of enduring grand narratives. My list of Lyotard's grand narratives in Table 2.1 therefore includes Lyotard's *Postmodern Condition* as a grand narrative and nine grand narratives that Lyotard touches upon in *The Postmodern Condition: A Report on Knowledge* (1979/1984). He is more in depth about 1, 3, and 5 through 9, while 2 and 4 are but briefly mentioned (see his sections 9 and 10). In sum, to demonstrate grand narrative analyses I shall here and there deconstruct Lyotard's grand narrative.

Essentializing analysis of grand narratives

Enlightenment is man's emergence from his self-incurred immaturity.

(Kant as cited in Best, 1995: 13).

Lyotard rejects grand narratives for their essentializing moves. An essentialism is a micro theory, an appeal to a fundamental essential of human, animal or world character. For example, Lyotard contends that cybernetic systems theory, Marxism and the Frankfurt School grand narratives have a model of society as a 'giant machine' (1979/1984: 13).

Instead of dismissing the grand narrative, a (critical) essentializing analysis can be used to juxtapose local stories with an official narrative. This is what I did in my Disney analysis (Boje, 1995). I argued that Walt is depicted in official corporate stories as the essential character of the creative genius and entrepreneur, who personifies the American Dream. Beneath Disney Theater is the cartoon factory with jobs organized according to division of labour, use of cheap labour under close supervision, a pyramid of functionally managed departments with gang bosses, speed bosses, repair bosses and inspectors, and finally, the suppression of all craft autonomy with predetermined schedules, formulas and interchangeable tasks. In more local stories Walt was Der Fuhrer, Mr Fear, Simon Legree, Ebeneezer Scrooge, Beelzebub the Devil and Mickey Mou$e. Essentializing narratives present Walt as saintly, and on Disney Sunday Theater as an easy-going, grandfatherly character. But, by many alternative accounts, Walt was intense, moody, vengeful, and used scare tactics in his story meetings. He would drum his fingers on his chair to intimidate a presenter to speed up or slow down a presentation. By including both essentialist and counter-traits you get a more balanced rendering than in official tales.

Lyotard's analysis proceeds by pointing out where society is not one 'integrated whole' and is not 'homogeneous' (1979/1984: 13) and is used to reject grand narratives 1 to 4 and 6 to 8. To accomplish his essentializing-rejection analysis Lyotard invokes Nietzsche's dissensus and atomized model of circular history (see 4, Table 2.1), but more often turns to John Searle's [a disciple of J.L. Austin] speech act theory (Lyotard, 1979/1984: footnote 34) and Wittgenstein's language games (p. 10). Ironically, Derrida and Searle have had well-known debates of 'the intentionality fallacy' of the pure speech act, upon which Lyotard bases his essentialist critique of essentialism (see Derrida, 1977/1989; Kamuf, 1991: 81). In short, Lyotard can be critiqued from enacting an 'essentialist' analysis of essentialism that rejects rather than balances (or otherwise rewrites) the grand narrative. 'Against such apodictic and dogmatic essentialist positing, one could argue that the social bond involves social relations, needs, sympathetic attractions, and libidinal bonds as well as language' (Best and Kellner, 1991: 177).

Universalizing analysis of grand narratives

Universals are grand principles, laws, totalizing truths and norms that gloss over narrative differences. Universalizing grand narratives are legitimating apologetics for particular visions of past or future and decisions on who decides and who knows what is knowledge. Lyotard defines legitimation as 'the process by which a "legislator" dealing with scientific discourse is authorized to prescribe the stated conditions ... determining whether a statement is to be included in that discourse for consideration by the scientific community' (1979/1984: 8).

For example, in my Disney study (1995), universalism is defined as an historical account that privileges one relatively narrow point of view or grand principle that glosses over differences in other stories. Disney storytelling is analysed for its control apparatus, how storytelling is used to embellish Disney philosophy by conveying codes of behaviour while obscuring their hegemonic construction. With deconstruction we pull on one of the strings of a universalized account and unravel the traces of its construction. A trace is like a foot print, or the trail a jet has left in the sky. Even though we do not see a constructor, we can tell one has passed by. Local stories resist the totalizing of an account into *'the' one and only story*. Stories are shaped to sell particular visions of past or future. Walt's vision was the 'G' movie and a theme park that would appeal to Midwestern America. All facets of the Disney operation 'synergized' around these principles. Cartoons and movies generated the characters that became theme rides and icons to merchandise products of all description. Again the analysis of the grand narrative of Midwestern America and the America dream is to trace other sides of the story and end with a resituation. Disney, for example, constructs its story as an act of domination to other sides of 'the' story.

Lyotard, however employs universalism analysis to reject logical positivism, imperial politics, German idealism, Marxism, Frankfurt School, cybernetic systems theory and post-industrial capitalism grand narratives (e.g. 1979/1984: 11–14). While there are many fun areas to deconstruct, the point, I think is to resituate, not to dismiss what remain as dominant narratives of organization life. For example, German idealism is viewed by Lyotard as a 'project of totalization, which was already present in Fichte and Schelling in the form of the idea of the System' and 'there is a universal "history" of the spirit, sprit is "life," and "life" is its own self-presentation and formulation in the ordered knowledge of all of its forms contained in the empirical sciences' (1979/1984: 34). Lyotard's analysis of this grand narrative is the narrator becomes a metasubject, history becomes idealized as the narration of an encyclopaedia of (hi)story, justifying its knowledge legitimacy by invoking a 'principle of usefulness' in an 'epic story of its emancipation' (1979/1984: 34–6).

Foundationalism analysis of grand narratives
Foundationalism may seem similar to essentialism and universalism analysis, but has some important differences. Universalism searches for a universal structure, essentialism quests for essential traits, but foundationalism is 'the impossible dream of attaining a foundation for knowledge, an absolute bedrock of truth [objectivity and reason] that could serve as the guarantee of philosophical systems' (Best and Kellner, 1991: 21, 207). Poststructuralists and postmodernists are critical of originary, first starting point foundations of knowledge including Husserl's claims for pure uncogitated phenomenological mediation and Austin's pure speech acts. Derrida (1976) calls this dream of foundations to language and knowledge the 'metaphysics of presence' in Western binary oppositions (see Chapter 1) that promises subjects unmediated access to reality. Plato, Descartes, Kant and Husserl had such a dream. Besides Derrida's duality deconstruction, another analysis of foundationalist grand narratives is Deleuze and Guattari's (1987) 'rhizomatics'. Instead of foundational reality: 'rhizomatics affirms the principles excluded from Western thought and reinterprets reality as dynamic, heterogeneous, and non-dichotomous' (Best and Kellner, 1991: 99). Deleuze and Guattari are concerned that a quest for foundational authority 'provides a fertile ground for fascism and authoritarian governments' (Best and Kellner, 1991: 231). For Lyotard the concern is intellectual terrorism.

While Lyotard repeatedly rejects Habermas' dream of foundational knowledge to ground his theoretical system of consensus, ideal speech community and communicative action – a more fruitful analysis would be to resituate it in a logic of rhizomatic differences. Laclau and Mouffe (1987) also argue that there are positive aspects of the Enlightenment foundationalist narratives, such as the dream of democratic discourse. Many reject such foundations of knowledge as God, Reason and laws of History, as progress myths, but there could be foundations worth resituating. Mouffe (1988) rejects the common critique of postmodern analysis, that a deconstruction of foundational knowledge makes one's work relativist. As Best and Kellner (1991: 199) summarize, 'within a particular moral tradition one can draw distinctions between just and unjust actions and principles and criticize exercises of arbitrary power.'

Lyotard invokes foundationalist analysis to reject every foundationalist dream quest. However, a rhizomatic analysis would merely decentre the one foundation into multiple, divergent and heterogeneous systems and semiotic dimensions. Rather than reject the foundationalist dream, Deleuze and Guattari emphasize the 'materiality of desire and rhizomatic linkages of thought to the world of flows' (Best and Kellner, 1991: 99). Finally, feminists (Hutcheon, 1989; Fraser and Nicholson, 1990; Flax, 1990) are not so eager to reject all foundationalism. Deconstructing it reveals the privileging of male patriarchy and hierarchy while marginalizing women to inferior power positions. Resituation rather than rejection allows democratic freedoms, human rights and equality to be reauthored without gender domination.

Progress myth of history analysis of grand narratives
Lyotard (1979/1984) critiques the post-industrial grand narrative for presenting a scenario of computerization and miniaturization as a progress myth while ignoring 'the continued failure to solve the world's energy problems' (p. 7) and the alienation resulting from withdrawing regulation-control 'from administrators and entrust[ing it] to machines' and to 'experts' (p. 14). He terms this 'the general paradigm of progress in science and technology, to which economic growth and the expansion of sociopolitical power seem to be natural complements' (p. 7). He also critiques the cybernetic systems theory grand narrative for presenting an optimistic self-regulating theory of progress and performativity whose only option is 'entropy' (p. 11–12). Function and dysfunction (strike or revolution) contribute to systemic progress. And he critiques Marxism as a grand narrative of functionalist class struggle to achieve progress and the 'optimization of its performance' (p. 12). Lyotard's critique of the progress myth as a grand narrative rests on pointing out that it is a truism and fallacious since 'scientific knowledge does not represent the totality of knowledge: it has always existed in addition to, and in competition and conflict with, another kind of knowledge, which I will call narrative in the interest of simplicity' (p. 7). In short, he critiques the progress myth for its

duality of 'scientific' versus 'narrative' knowing (see Chapter 1). He refers to this as a speculative grand narrative with roots in Hegel (pp. 33–4, 38) and Kant (p. 32). Only with a linear theory of time, do we assume each move in history brings about more enlightened corporate behaviour.

Network analysis of grand narratives
Lyotard asserts that 'no self is an island' and that the self is embedded in nodal circuits of flat networks of inquiry (p. 15). Each self 'exists in a fabric of relations that is now more complex and mobile than every before' (p. 15). As in my Tamara theatrics metaphor for Disney each story is an inter-textual framing of reality being chased by wandering and fragmenting groups of spectators. Each story masks a diversity of voices. The post-modern analysis breaks away from the fixed stage, the mono-voice and the universal story line. Tamara is open conversation in a multiplicity of minor stories that collectively constitute, transform and reform the theatrics of the storytelling organization.

While Lyotard dismisses grand narratives as fictitious and incredulous, he also posits a postmodern science (1979/1984: 54–66). He observes that Newtonian physics has given way to quantum mechanics and Einstein relativity theory, that total proofs are impossible with Godel's theorem, notes the emergence of Thom's catastrophe theory, schizophrenia, double bind and paradox. And his list is similar in many respects to Best and Kellner's (1997) Chapter 5 on postmodern science. However, Best and Kellner go further in identifying complexity, chaos theory and self-organizing systems. While they too reject the mechanistic machine meta-phors and reductionism of many of the grand narratives, they are careful not to reject all grand narrative. 'While inorganic systems are subject to entropy and ultimately demise, organic systems are open to countervailing and counterentropic forces. Life according to this view is self-perpetuating and self-organizing, seeking to expand, develop, and unfold, often in sur-prising and novel ways' (p. 210). Postmodern sciences resituates the grand narratives in the life of nature.

Paul Cilliers (1998) adopts Lyotard uncritically for it links complexity and chaos theory. What is pioneering about Cilliers' work is the way he builds upon Lyotard's theory of the self embedded in networks of dis-course communities as a way to respond to the common criticism that postmodern is relativistic and has no platform to compare one argument as more or less valid or ethical than any other. Each narrative claim argues Cilliers can be assessed locally in the context of its linked speech commu-nities. Again, the argument would be more solid if Lyotard's rejection of all grand narrative was tempered as in the Best (1995) and Best and Kellner (1991, 1997) treatments. The next four analyses are suggested in Best and Kellner's critiques of Lyotard.

Big story analysis of grand narratives
Grand narratives 1 through 3 and 6 through 9 (Table 2.1) appear to sub-sume every story into one totalizing narrative. But within these and in

other texts, there are 'Big stories' about 'the rise of capital, patriarchy, or the colonial subject' (Best and Kellner, 1991: 172). The distinction between big story and grand narrative is an important one since many macro-social, political, economic and cultural theories tell highly complex stories with many rhizomatic relations. Foucault's archaeology and genealogical analysis of knowledge are two examples. Burrell's (1997) *Pandemonium* and Bauman's (1989) *Modernity and the Holocaust* are two more.

Synchronic and diachronic analyses of grand narratives

Synchronic narratives tell stories about a specific society at one time in history while diachronic narratives analyse 'historical change, discon-tinuities, and ruptures' (Best and Kellner, 1991: 172). It takes a diversity of narratives, synchronic and diachronic to tell the stories of the world of heterogeneous organizations and cultures. I agree with Best and Kellner (1991: 177) that Lyotard does tend to lump too many narrative types together and dismiss them all as essentializing, foundationalist and uni-versalizing grand narratives.

Empowering and disempowering analysis of grand narratives

There is an important difference between empowering and disempower-ing grand narratives. Fundamentalist, ultra-conservative, fascist and idealist narratives need critical and skeptical analysis, and incredulity. However, there are narratives of democracy, equality, sustainability and social justice that are life affirming and empowering. And the two types, empowering and disempowering, do intertwine and appropriate the others' rhetorical stances.

Restorying analysis of grand narratives

Take them apart, reconstruct and rewrite them argues Best and Kellner. 'We would argue', say Best and Kellner 'that just because some narratives of legitimation are highly dubious, politically suspect, and unconvincing does not entail that we should reject *all* grand narratives – that is, all traditional philosophy and all social theory which has systematic and comprehensive aims' (1991: 176–7). White and Epston (1990: 15–17) argue that a 'dominant story' or grand narrative ignores and marginalizes experiences that fall outside of its domain, and may not provide space for the performance of one's preferred (local) stories. A form of resistance to grand narratives is therefore not only to resituate the dominant grand narrative, but to 'restory' in ways that reauthor the lives of the tellers. (See Boje, 1998c, 1999a for a review of restorying and organization narratives.) In sum:

1. Rather than reject all grand narratives, it is possible to resituate and restory them using the analyses described.
2. Rather than put all grand narratives into the modern camp, we can recognize that there are premodern, modern and postmodern writers who seek to critique and/or reform various grand narratives. My own preference (1995) is to see organizations as a hybrid of premodern,

modern and postmodern grand and petit narratives and stories. At one extreme, a storytelling organization such as Disney, can oppress by subordinating everyone and collapsing everything to one 'grand narrative' or 'grand story'. The official story is what Walt said or what Eisner now says. At the other extreme, the storytelling organization can be a pluralistic construction of a multiplicity of stories, storytellers and story performance events that are like Tamara but are realized differently depending upon the stories in which one is participating. An antenarrative perspective traces the interplay of both.

3. I support Jameson's (1991: 123) observation that organizations do not follow a course of era-to-era displacement, but rather that discursive elements shift in emphasis and in priority. There is an inconsistency in Lyotard's analysis of rejecting grand narratives while positing a 'postmodern condition' as its linear replacement.

4. It appears that there are simultaneous grand narratives, some empowering and others quite disempowering. For example, Ub and the other artists resisted Walt's attempts to implement Frederick Taylor's (1911) rationalistic principles of scientific management. Yet, it is a discipline legitimated in grand narratives 1 and 8 in Table 2.1.

5. Within the Enlightenment narratives there is the antenarrative of contending perspectives ranging from rejection, reform and salvage to restorying.

6. Rather than reject grand narratives, we can juxtapose alternative big and little stories and trace their interplay in the 'flowing soup' (Weick, 1995: 128).

7. We need not confuse essentialism, universalism and foundationalism analysis with grand narratives. And some essence, universal and foundation Enlightenment such as spirituality, ecology and democracy could be worth hanging onto. Some foundations count: for Dave Iwerks, the son of Ub Iwerks, Walt's once-upon-a-time partner, it was Ub not Walt that created Mickey.

8. Each grand narrative covers a multitude of storied antenarrative variations. There are differences between official and non-official stories, between CEO and non-CEO stories (e.g. Boje, 1995).

9. We need to analyse the differences between macrostory and microstory. At the macrostory level, each big story is one consensus, one totalizing account, one set of universals, one set of essential foundations and one construction. One side of a story masks other sides, and without context, we can miss what is between the lines of a story. To analyse, resituate and restory grand narratives, then, is to let a thousand stories bloom rather than dismiss certain stories as unworthy. The relation of microstoria and macrostory is the subject of Chapter 3.

3

Microstoria analysis

The Italians are doing the important work in *microstoria analysis* (also called microhistory). Microstoria is an antenarrative analysis due to its open history approach and its skepticism of grand narratives of macrohistory. 'The purpose of microhistory,' says Muir (1991: cci), 'is to elucidate historical causation on the level of small groups where most of real life takes place and to open history to peoples who would be left out by other methods.' Causality is the subject of Chapter 6. Microstorians want to call into question grand narratives of macrohistory, particularly elite great man histories by collecting 'little people' microstories. They contrast microstoria to macrohistory or grand narrative analysis that they assume is limiting in the ten ways I summarize in Table 3.1.

Instead of the unitary, totalizing and universal grand narratives of history we reviewed in Chapter 2, the focus of this chapter is on identifying incoherence, discontinuity, contradictions and ruptures in everyday life. Instead of teleology of progress, microstorians focus on the excluded narratives of women, ethnic minorities, witches, day labourers, peasants, charlatans and other 'little people'. Instead of great man grand narratives of *the* hegemony of a unitary macrohistory, the point is to create many histories from below.

Microstorians boldly question both the grand narratives of capitalism and Marxism. There is no Enlightenment faith that reason or science has progressively liberated human beings. Rather there is an effort to reclaim local ways of knowing delegitimated by macrohistory, science and progress, and development myths. Microstoria relies upon systematic archival analysis from property registries, notary records, ecclesiastical archives, trial proceedings, pamphlets, etc. The clues of non-elite persons and places are traced to reconstruct everyday life and to explore matrimonial strategies, clashes of subordinated and dominant classes, etc. through the investigation of 'exceptional' cases. Microstoria is what is termed 'prosopography from below'. That is the quantitative study of social networks and the qualitative system of non-elites in a series of microstories. The narratives are selected and analysed not for their statistical frequency, but because they constitute the 'apparently exceptional' (Muir, 1991: 7). Table 3.1 gives a brief chapter overview.

Table 3.1 *Microstoria assumptions, trace analysis and a middle ground*

Microstoria assumptions

1. Unitary and universalizing macrohistory narrative is untenable.
2. Abstract formal theories of grand narrative event-structures do not hold up when tested against the concrete reality of small-scale life.
3. Great man histories that totalize 'little people' histories into one macrosocietal narrative of power without margins are suspect.
4. Local ways of knowing rendered illegitimate by declaring them demonic, criminal, heretical, unscientific or dead can be reclaimed.
5. Discontinuities, contradictions and ruptures in everyday life epitomize the other side of the story of macrohistorical narratives of harmony.
6. Progress through science and technology is called into question by looking at human costs of modernization.
7. Unknown microhistories can be rescued from oblivion through archival analysis.
8. History is a multifaceted flow of microstories with multi-centres.
9. A pre-existing social and natured reality exists outside the text that is more than social construction perspectivism or poststructural deconstruction.
10. Between macro logical-deduction and grounded theory-induction is the abduction method of microstoria analysis.

Trace in microstoria analysis

1. Tracing name networks in microstoria networks.
2. Tracing clues like a Sherlock Holmes detective.
3. Tracing micro-survivals in spite of dominant culture.
4. Tracing the middle ground of microstoria and grand narrative.

Middle ground between micro and macrostory

1. Macrohistories of social, organization and global transformations coexist with microstories of discontinuity and multiple centres.
2. Microstories of subordinated individuals supplement and reciprocate macrosocietal and cultural narratives of the dominant classes.
3. There are pockets of resistance and survival of microstoria embedded in the dominance of elite macro-societal narratives.
4. Multinational corporate accounts of macro-economic and societal history can be redefined through microstoria.
5. The microstories of the local take place within the context of media-promoted grand narratives of political, economic and social change.

Microstoria has its own epistemology and ontology

Microstoria is not based on theories of social construction, nihilistic perspectivism or even the story deconstruction work we looked at in Chapter 1. It is also decidedly contrary to the grand narrative positions of Chapter 2, but is not just the abandonment of grand narrative as Lyotard proposes. As I see it, microstoria explores the vast middle ground between grand narrative (as well as macrohistory) and postmodernist concern for local narratives. It is less abandonment than a calling into question of the distortions of elite narratives by reconstituting exceptional antenarratives or microstories and using systematic archival procedure within the time's political, social and economic context.

I shall briefly explore how microstoria analysis is neither grand narrative analysis or story deconstruction analysis, nor is it the 'thick description' of Clifford Geertz's cultural harmony (1973) or Glaser and Strauss's (1967) 'grounded theory' of inductive ethnography. An important point here is that microstorians do not see themselves subsumed under grounded theory. To figure out what microstoria is, we can look at what it is not.

Not deconstruction

There is narrative analysis of this middle ground, but it is not deconstruction. Indeed the best known of the microstorians Carlo Ginzburg (1980) is against deconstruction and post-Foucauldian deconstructionists in particular. Ginzburg definitely argues for an outside reading of the meaning of the text that is more than mere possibility. 'They [microstorians] insist that the historian deals with a real subject matter' and a material textuality (Iggers, 1997: 108). To understand this reservation, we need to look more closely at what it means to be outside a text.

Microstorians assume there is a pre-existing social and natured reality outside the text. 'Il n'y a pas de-hors-texte' is Derrida's most misinterpreted slogan (see Chapter 1). Marc Currie says in *Postmodern Narrative* it 'does not mean there is nothing outside the text as most commentators have taken it. It is closer to "There is no outside-text"' (1998: 45). Language, says Currie '*is* a material practice not only in the sense that it is to be understood in isolation from the mind as the material marks of writing but also in the sense that textual and linguistic constructs are (to use a word that Derrida avoids) *reified* or transformed into material things and practices in the world' (1998: 90). The outside reading of organization is impossibility (Currie, 1998: 47). It is impossible for two reasons: (1) intertextuality, and (2) outside-text is another text. Intertextuality (see Chapter 5) 'posits a model of referentiality which cannot distinguish between reference to the world and reference to another text, since textuality is woven into all' (Currie, 1998: 70). Yet, there is more than a possible misinterpretation of 'outside-text' going on here, the microstorians are against deconstruction for other reasons.

Ginzburg adopts a positivistic notion of 'truth' that he acknowledges for Derrida would be a heresy:

> I am deeply interested in catching the right meaning – I know that is a kind of heresy for a lot of people, that notion of right meaning. But I am deeply against every kind of Derrida trash, that kind of cheap skeptical attitude .... I am deeply against it. I start with a kind of realistic attitude in the sense of a realistic notion of truth in some way, but at the same time, I am conscious of the fact that there are no rules that can be taken for granted .... So maybe there is a contradiction between that, the fact that I start with that positivistic notion of truth, but at the same time, I am strongly against an positivistic naivete about knowledge. (Ginzburg as cited in Muir, 1991: xxv)

Not exactly thick description

Microstorians are also quick to point out that they are not doing a Clifford Geertz version of 'thick description'. While there are affinities, such as the focus on small groups, detailed/dense descriptions, and scaled down history, there are important differences between microstoria and Geertz's work. In particular 'Geertz's claim that he deals with a world on a small scale' is for microstorians a macrosocial theory of culture as 'an integrated whole' (Iggers, 1997: 110). Microstorians are focusing more on the disunity, the ways in which one class opposes or resists another. Glaser and Strauss (1967: 144–7) offer a critique of Geertz's approach to thick description, showing how it does not meet all the criteria for constant comparison. At issue is how Geertz's concern to validate/invalidate a particular grand theory of Weberian rationalization is steering what gets sampled for observation. His theoretical framework limits his ability to trace the more dynamic aspects of the people he is studying. 'He is willing to generate theory, but stopped himself because he took the opposition's view too seriously; and also because, as an anthropologist, he could perhaps not quite let go of the propensity not to generalize without great ethnographic detail about the society' (1967: 147). At issue here is that the accounts appear more integrated than may be the case. To the microstorians, the issue however, is not to compare a set of historical narratives or archival data with some contemporary theory. The approach is radically different from such objectives in grounded theory. Rather, the microstorians want to think, feel and see the world the way it was seen in that time and place. Microstoria prefers a polysemic reading of symbols with a focus on the dynamics of cultural differentiation that runs counter to more functional interpretative approaches. As Iggers (1997: 104) summarizes Geertz's approach to thick description 'does not give us access to an individual but only to the culture in which he or she is bound up' (1997: 104).

Not quite marxist

Indeed the best known of the microstorians Carlo Ginzburg (1980) is against deconstruction and post-Foucauldian deconstructionists in particular. While Foucault's genealogical approach shares much in common with microstoria, it differs in a significant way. To the microstorians Foucault is using the genealogy of prisons, clinics, etc. to look at how contemporary concepts like 'punishment' and 'prison' have changed their situated meaning and usage over time. However, for the microstorians the task is not to critique or amplify contemporary theory, it is to see the world through the eyes and mindset of the Other. Ginzburg definitely argues for an outside, even empirical reading of the meaning of the text that is more than mere possibility and more than social or postmodern construction. 'They [microstorians] insist that the historian deals with a real subject matter' (Iggers, 1997: 108). While rejecting Marxist macrohistory narratives, the microstorians retain a post-Marxist focus on ideological hegemony, social and economic inequality, and material conditions of power.

We can now put the difference with Marx together with the difference with Geertz. Levi (1992: 100–5) points out two important differences between this post-Marxist approach and that of thick description:

1.A.   **Relativity and idealism** – The only thing we can do is to first try to grasp and then make explicit, via thick description, the probable meaning of actions. Adherents of this approach do not believe it necessary to question the limitations, possibilities and measurability of rationality itself. Any such inherent limitations or confines are, rather, assumed to be set by the endless game of essentially unevaluable interpretations veering between idealism and relativism instead of being assessed by the standard of some definite conception of human rationality.

1.B.   **Homogeneous or heterogeneous sign meaning** – It seems to me that one of the main differences of perspective between microhistory and interpretive anthropology is that the latter sees a homogeneous meaning in public signs and symbols whereas microhistory seeks to define and measure them with reference to the multiplicity of social representations they produce .... For [microstoria] in the context of differing social conditions, these symbolic structures produce a fragmented and differentiated multiplicity of representations; and it is these which should be the object of out study.

2.   **Symbolism is presented as a single universal sign system** – Geertz concludes by proposing a tentative use of general, academic conceptualization only to revitalize the concepts in the concrete examples of thick descriptions. In this way a repertoire of concepts is woven into a repertoire of interpreted events in the hope that they will work together so that simple events may be made scientifically eloquent and conversely that far-reaching conclusions may be drawn from the density of simple facts.

In sum, the ontological approach of microstoria is one in which there is knowledge that is specific to time and place, that can be read in the material remains of stories recorded in various archives and diaries. What is antenarrative is the focus on entering the webs of storied relationships and meanings, the stories and counter-stories of that time. The mindset is radically different from and resists being collapsible to contemporary thought. However, the ontology, the way of seeing the dynamics of the world is post-Marxist, seeing the hegemonic forces of class that define subject positions. In this sense it has not given up all grand narrative. However, various power elites, how local mystics and witches endured religious repression, and how a local knowledge persisted in the face of more hegemonic forces. Grand narrative is interpenetrated here and there with local accounts, with microstories of how people have resisted domination.

What is microstoria's epistemology?

Microstorian work is more akin to Charles Sanders Peirce's semiotic theory of 'abduction' and Michel Bakhtin's theory of carnival. Microstorians assume that between macro logical-deduction and grounded theory-induction is the abduction method of microstoria analysis (see below for definitions and contrasts).

I will focus this chapter on how microstorians use 'trace' in several important ways (see Table 3.1). As I proceed I will show how their use of 'trace' is different from Derridian deconstruction-trace. For this introduction suffice it to say that microstoria analysis is rooted in the epistemology of Charles Sanders Peirce and in particular tracing stranded relations in situated historical contexts and in the concept of 'abduction' as opposed to either 'induction' or 'deduction'.

Recall that logical deduction seeks to verify *a priori* formal theory, while induction or grounded theory focuses on generating theory from *in situ* observations (see Chapter 8 for more on inductive and deductive analysis). Examples of formal theory from which deductive hypotheses are tested are Weber's ideal types of authority (bureaucratic, charismatic and feudalistic), Marx's labour process and surplus value theories, and Durkheim's typology of mechanistic and organic social solidarity. Peirce gives the example of trying to deduce as a man who believes in the infallibility of the Pope.

> For example, suppose the hypothesis to be that a man believes in the infallibility of the Pope. Then if we ascertain in any way that he believes in the immaculate conception, in the confessional, and in prayers for the dead, or on the other hand that he disbelieves all or some of these things, either fact will be almost decisive of the truth or falsity of the proposition. Such inference is *deduction*. (1955: 153)

A narrative approach that relies more upon deduction is Fisher's (1984, 1985a, b) 'narrative paradigm theory' (NPT). NPT seeks to ascertain the believability of a story by deductive means.

An example of inductive, grounded, thick description theory is Geertz's observations of Balinese cock fighting (1973, 1988). The hypotheses and theory concepts are systematically grounded in the way data are collected and analysed. Peirce gives the following example of an inductive hypothesis study:

> For example, suppose that I have been led to surmise that among our coloured population there is a greater tendency toward female births than among our whites. I say, if that be so, the last census must show it. I examine the last census report and find that, sure enough, there was a somewhat greater proportion in that census year. To accord a certain faith to my hypothesis on that account is legitimate. It is a strong induction. (1955: 152)

Abduction

Peirce observed that scientists do something that often is neither deduction nor induction. It is an inferential, intuitive guess that he called abduction

(Peirce, 1955: 150–6). Both induction and deduction also involve a certain amount of guesswork, but Peirce wanted to study what we now call the ethnomethodology of scientific inference. Peirce, writing between 1896 and 1908, explained it this way:

> At each stage of his long investigation, Kepler has a theory which is approximately true, since it approximately satisfies the observations ... and he proceeds to modify this theory, after the most careful and judicious reflection in such a way as to render it more rational or closer to the observed fact .... Kepler shows his keen logical sense in detailing the whole process by which he finally arrived at the true orbit. This is the greatest piece of Retroductive [abductive] reasoning ever performed. (1955: 155–6)

Abductive narrative inquiry can be seen in a careful reading of Glaser and Strauss's *Discovery of Grounded Theory* (1967: 102). However, it is not in the whole theory, but in one of its constructs: 'constant comparison'. They indicate the purpose of 'constant comparative' methods is to do the ethnographic data collection, coding and analysis as you go, rather than to collect a lot of observations, interviews or surveys then code it once and for all to prove or disprove a deductive hypothesis. This is a danger in narrative work: to collect everything and then to try to code it the way one does in survey analysis. Pre-post test works well to verify theory *a priori* deductive frameworks but not to question them or to generate inductive theories. And in narrative analysis, where an emic or inductive typology is being sought/created, the work of constant comparisons is essential. Glaser and Strauss saw constant comparative method as also between deduction and grounded-induction.

The hazard in both deduction and induction is 'exampling' stories by finding grounded cases or inventing stories to confirm and fit the analyst's elucidation of a logically deduced theory (Glaser and Strauss, 1967: 5). The specific issue is one of taking stories out-of-context. Interviews for example, can be occasions where the situation elicits a story and is different from a story that emerges from the situation-at-work with its entire *in situ* performance context. Story and context are intertextual and interpenetrating. The middle ground that Glaser and Strauss (1967) call 'constant comparative analysis' is similar but not identical to what Peirce terms 'abduction'. In narrative work, it involves collecting narratives in the situation of their performance as opposed to a call to construct a story or to re-enact a story for the narrative researcher.

In constant comparison analysis stories are chosen systematically through sampling frames (e.g. types of people, times, places, etc.). Stories are then comparatively analysed as the research unfolds to give theoretical control over theory building and verification.

Peirce has a looser middle ground between induction and deduction, between gathering stories and verifying theory. Peirce uses the term 'abduction' to describe an ongoing inquiry situation where scientists have a more spontaneous creative insight they speculate may be tied to their data, or they select one among several plausible hypotheses. And it is this middle ground that is of concern to microstorians.

In sum, the microstorians focus on recovering forgotten and marginalized history through both quantitative and qualitative study. While they focus on the grounded emergent micro-aspects of stories, they also situate those stories within the grander narrative schemes of the time, such as class, race and socioeconomic moorings. The analysis focuses upon identifying names of places of people in ways that allow microstories to be told. Microstoria is sensitive to the micropolitics of power, the middle ground between local and grand narrative, and treats historical material as real. As such it is not a deconstructive analysis and it is not the harmony-seeking micro-culture work of grounded theory (with the exception of constant comparisons). At the same time the interpretative inquiry is based in abduction to interrogate the gap, contradictions and disjuncture between what was said and what was recorded and between the preconceptions of elites and exotic characters. In the next section I will examine different ways in which 'trace' is used in microstoria analysis.

Doing microstoria in organization studies

I will look at tracing names, clues, survivals and the middle ground between micro and macro narrative.

Tracing names in microstoria networks
In microstoria analysis, tracing the names of individuals enmeshed in networks of social relationships gives the narrative analyst some access to ideas and images of the past. Edward Muir in selections from *Quaderni Storici*, an Italian journal of microstoria, puts it this way:

> The lines that converge upon and diverge from the name, creating a kind of closely woven web, provides for the observer a graphic image of the network of social relationships into which the individual is inserted. (1991: ix)

Muir calls this graphic network image 'propography' and amplifies the trace of names in networks of more names in footnote 13 with a quote from Ferone and Firpo:

> An attempt, to clarify all the complex density and the think network of connections and relations that lie tangled together in facts, real situations, events, ideas, images, men, and social groups of the past. (1986: 521, cited in Muir, 1991: xxiii)

Tracing the names named (both men and women) creates an analysis of microstories that thickly describe what I would like to call the 'microstoria network'. It is the tracing of a 'propography from below' of little people tangled in a storied web of events, images and ideas. In the microstoria network each node is an individual and each relationship is a story of images and ideas linking them to other individuals.

Tracing clues like a Sherlock Holmes detective

In the search for the lost past, clues are traces not about the big lives of generals, presidents of CEOs but instead the focus is on the everyday life of 'little people'. And the focus is even narrower on very obscure clues. Microstoria analysts sift through the historical testimonies of little people in documents and records that macrohistory analysts disregard as quite insignificant to telling the grand narratives of history. For example, in Ginzburg's work, it is tracing 'participants misunderstandings of each other [that] offers clues to now-lost ways of thinking' (Muir, 1991: x). In Ginzburg's (1980) best-known work *The Cheese and the Worms* we read stories of a sixteenth-century Italian miller named Menocchio. Ginzburg traces clues of how Menocchio 'creatively misread' an odd collection of books including the Koran to create an errant cosmology. By tracing these clues of misreading Ginzburg recaptures a forgotten material peasant cultural philosophy.

Here is a good place to point out that the microstoria analysts differentiate their history work from the genealogical approach of Michel Foucault. While both approaches look to documentary evidence, Foucault resituates the present in the past in ways that microstoria detectives find objectionable. Microstoria work is more akin to Ivan Illich, the premodernist than to postmodern aspects of Foucault's genealogical approach. Illich (1993: 3–4), for example, in *In the Vineyard of the Text: A Commentary to Hugh's Didascalicon* does what I would call microstoria analysis.

I will illustrate with a microstory of my own. When I met Ivan Illich on Tuesday February first in 1996, I asked him to sign his book for me. He signed it on page 26 rather than the front of the book, like most authors I know. And he underlined footnote 26 which is in Latin but the underlined phrase is 'Charity never ends.'

To understand this gesture you need to have some context. Illich purposely avoids the modern language and categories of the past 450 years so he can look at and I think live the time around 1150 before technical breakthroughs like Guttenberg's moveable type changed how people looked at reading and books. High of Saint Victor's text *Didascalicon* is for Illich a forgotten text that gives us clues to pre-textual cultures of the monastery and scholarly university. Illich asks what is the symbolic impact of a new thirteenth-century technology in the context of Hugh's age.

Context matters. In Hugh's time, you could not read unless you did it out loud by mumbling the words. If you wanted to punish a monk you made them be silent, because in silence people could not read a text. Reading had to be accompanied by mumbling and was usually done in mumbling rooms with other people. In the Jewish tradition, you rock your body to understand. This was also true of Hugh's time, but more important than body reading was mumbling.

New pagination technology transformed reading into a silent act, into something mental. And it is Hugh that is one of the advocates of the new technology. 'Hugh asks the reader to expose himself to the light emanating from the pate, *ut agnoscat seipsum*, so that he may recognize himself, acknowledge his self' (Illich, 1993: 21). The 'self' is for Illich 'one of the greatest discoveries of the twelfth century' (1993: 23). And this discovery is made possible by a new way of thinking about text. The page becomes a mirror; a way to reflect the self and reading becomes an act of sight, no longer the sound of mumbling scholars and monks. The office, function or role denotes for earlier medievals person. Hugh instructs his students in reading 'to a seek out the sayings of a wise person, and to ardently strive to keep them ever before the eyes of their mind, as a mirror before their face' (Hugh as quoted in Illich, 1993: 25). The mirror survives as Rorty's work points out. With this context, perhaps you can trace the significance to me of the 'clue' that Illich left in his book signature. And not his signature, but my name was written on that page.

When Hugh reads Illich says it is a 'pilgrimage at dawn through the vineyard of the page [that] leads toward paradise, which he conceives as a garden'. And the pages of that time were ornamented with vines and other images as a way to read and be connected to the life world. 'The words that he plucks form the trellis of the lines are a foretaste and a promise of the sweetness that is to come' (Illich, 1993: 26). For Hugh reading is friendship, a social act where Hugh says 'love and pursuit and something akin to the friendship of wisdom', motivate his pilgrimage (as cited in Illich, 1993: 26). And it is precisely here that footnote 53 appears and where Illich autographed his text not with his own name but with the words 'To David in LA. 2 1 – Tu 1996'. It is for me a significant clue that I have sought to understand ever since.

Tracing micro-survivals in spite of dominant culture

While microstoria analysis is not very concerned with explaining the present, I think their analysis can be turned to contemporary problems. For example, in the dominant or elite culture of the twentieth century, there are here and there traces of surviving popular cultures. For example, in Italy there are still craft guilds of artisans that survive in modern and late modern capitalism. Popular culture in this context is peasant, working-class or rural cultures. For example, Ginzburg's work with Menocchio microstories reconstructs the popular culture of a 'once perverse pantheism' (Muir, 1991: x) that survived in the more dominant (in numbers) Christian society. And Illich's work explores the twelfth-century cosmology of Hugh, but then returns to the present to juxtapose Hugh's worldview with our images of virtual texts and computer literacy.

It seems to me that if we in organizational studies only analyse organizations through the 'elite' stories of its CEOs, owners and managers, we miss the survivals of 'popular culture'. We could therefore study temporary employment, secretaries and janitors to get at alternative cosmologies of the workplace.

Tracing the middle ground of microstoria and grand narrative

While one may question grand narratives and macrohistory, it is does not seem prudent to reject what is all around us. Societies do put their history into grand narratives, mostly great man narratives. The challenge is to call these progress, Enlightenment and phallologocentric narratives into question. Nor does it make sense to me to do only grounded interpretative work that does not set that work in a context of social and economic theory. And this is more than interpretative relativism: the Holocaust did happen. Stories have a situated context. If we accept the microstoria assumptions in Table 3.1, then it seems that history is not unilinear or unitary. As Iggers argues 'There is no reason a history dealing with broad social transformations and one centering on individual existences cannot coexist and supplement each other' (1997: 104).

If we only focus on local stories without putting these accounts into broader social and economic contexts we risk the 'trivialization of history' (Iggers, 1997). I think that microstoria offers a way for organizational studies to move from CEO-histories of the great corporations to polyphonic histories. But microstoria cannot stand the critiques of methodological irrationalism and trivialization without a macrosocial context.

In closing, we have looked at several approaches to microstoria, tracing changes in the grand story, reclaiming narratives contrary to the story, and a middle ground analysis between macro and microstory. Microstory has the potential to trace acts of resistance of 'little people' to the grand narratives that embed their lives. While much of the Italian microstoria analyses reclaim narrative knowledge of the distant past there is no reason such analysis cannot contrast the less grand stories of official corporate history with local stories of resistance. Putting local 'little people' stories side by side with corporate and great-CEO narratives is one way to proceed.

The Columbus story example of microstoria analysis

The Christopher Columbus Story has become a grand narrative of the 'Great American Dream' that is being recently disputed by microstoria claims (Boje, 2000b). It is an important narrative to analyse since both proponents and detractors consider the Columbus Story a personification of global capitalism and corporate entrepreneurship. While the narrative analysts bringing forth the counter-claims are not microstoria Italians, they exhibit prototypical microstoria assumptions, use trace, but, some may argue, do not attempt any middle ground between macrohistorical and microstoria narrative analysis. I shall briefly review how previous historians and popular writers restory Christopher Columbus in ways that become an apologetic for corporate imperialism. By corporate imperialism, I mean the colonizing of what is left of the ecology and our everyday festive lives by monopolistic multinational corporate power spectacles, including short-term greed of the largest transnational corporations on the planet and the acts of ancient nation states (Boje, 2000b). The charge of race genocide in Columbus narrating is a serious one. The basic microstoria question is how people of one political economy construct a narrative belief system (racist ideology) that tells them they are better, higher, more advanced, more civilized, more evolved, more rightful owners than another political economy.

The Columbus narrative is a spectacle that invents its hero scripting stories and theatrics of the great journey as paths for future societies to emulate. With the hype of American nationalism, few people know what took place. And even when they question the hype, the narrating is sufficiently compelling that most seem to ignore the historical record. To many the Columbus narrative stands as the 'official' and 'true' histories and it does not much matter what has been accumulated in the way of historical records including Columbus's ship's logs, diaries of priests such as Bartolome de las Casas, and various others sojourners to the so-called 'new world'. There are several microstoria approaches taken to the analysis.

First approach: trace microhistories across the time span
of a grand narrative
As an example of the first approach, I want to summarize how Yewell (1992) looks at historical documents century by century to see how the Columbus Story has been rehistoricized. His work is consistent with microstoria assumptions one, two and three in Table 3.1. He uses the century by century documents to make the unitary and universalizing macrohistory of the Columbus narrative untenable. He challenges the basic event-structures of the Columbus narrative, asserting that they just do not hold up when tested against the concrete reality of small-scale life. Finally, he challenges the Columbus story as a great man history that totalizes 'little people' histories into one macrosocietal narrative.

In the first century (1492–1592) the story of Christopher Columbus was not the grandiose legend it is today. He was the 'errant sailor who brought to Europe news of lands to the west ... this knowledge [that] would dawn slowly on the rest of Europe over the course of the next few generations' (Yewell, 1992: 167). The legend was not widely known in Europe, so Martin Waldseemuller, a map maker gave the honour of discovery to Amerigo Vespucci who had written and disseminated his own claims of 'discovery' (Yewell, 1992: 168). Few, if any, paid any attention to the ship's logs of the Admiral's voyages or to de las Casas' journals.

In the second century (1592–1692) the Puritans began to settle the North American continent, pushing aside the natives as they proceeded. Native agriculture practices were paid no heed, since there were 'superior' Euro technologies and land-clearing methods that made more sense to settlers. Foreign animals and the Indians, also considered beasts, were exterminated without any moral dilemma whatsoever.

In the third century (1692–1792) the United States searched for White male heroes to put on pedestals for the tricentennial celebration. There were proposals to change the name to Columbia or the United States of Columbia. 'The Tammany Society, also known as the Colombian Order, had grown in part from the Sons of Liberty during the Revolution, and ironically claimed as its two guiding lights Columbus and Chief Tammany of the Delaware Indians, who had welcomed William Penn and his followers to their new colony in 1682 ... then in 1828, Columbus-mania broke out' (Yewell, 1992: 169).

In the fourth century (1792–1892) the Columbus Story that most people know today was crafted. Washington Irving created a fictional man to inhabit the myth and legitimate the spectacle of Columbus-mania. He wrote *The Life and Voyages of Columbus* (1828). Irving constructed a fictional account of the voyage (in comparison to ship logs and diaries of the day) and invented accounts of the mutineering crew, the fear that the world was flat, and the qualities of entrepreneurial White character and natives standing in the way of progress and commerce that stand firm as believed and unchangeable historical fact. Microstorians argue the story was designed to cater to the sentiments of Irving's day in order to rationalize the continued appropriation of lands, the genocide of 100 million natives throughout the Americas begun in 1492. Columbus-mania grew by leaps and bounds and the great man Columbus was shaped and outfitted as the main character and role model of the American Dream. On 24 February 1890, the House of Representatives had a Columbian Exposition. The massacre of Wounded Knee took place in December 1890 'with the West "won" and Columbus more than ever a symbol of the nation's vitality, planning for the Exposition was well underway' (Yewell, 1992: 170). The Pledge of Allegiance was written as part of the Columbian Exposition and circulated to schools across the land. The First Columbus Day was in 1866 in the Italian neighbourhoods of New York City. In 1869, other cities had their own unofficial celebrations. In 1882, the Knights of Columbus were founded in New Haven and the campaign to elect Columbus as the greatest of all American heroes drew more mania than ever before. President Benjamin Harrison declared 12 October 1892, a national holiday to commemorate Columbus. Future presidents would replicate his action.

In the fifth century (1892–1992) the Columbus story took on new spectacle proportions. In 1905, the governor of Colorado set aside a Columbus holiday, making it law in 1907. Other states followed suit and in 1937, President Franklin Roosevelt made it a national holiday. There were Wild West shows, dime novels of cowboys and Indians, and at the close of the century TV serials, motion pictures, textbooks, cartoons, Thanksgiving Day and Columbus Day spectacles were crafted to make it appear that pilgrims and Indians lived in a festival relationship. In 1989, President George Bush's Columbus Day Proclamation embellished the corporate aspects of the Columbus myth. The Columbus myth is made over into the legend of 'American entrepreneurs and business people' whom 'accepted great risks in order to pursue their dreams'. President Bush tells of the 'courageous navigator who discovered the Americas' a symbol of the 'generations of brave and bold Americans who, like him, have overcome great odds in order to chart the unknown' (1992: 200–1). With the movies *1492* and *Christopher Columbus*, a Hollywood Columbus is now the 'authentic' story and any version others put forward is measured against what is already to microstorians a fake.

Second approach: reclaim forgotten knowledge
A second approach to microstoria analysis of the Columbus Story starts with assumptions 4 to 9 in Table 3.1: that it is possible to confront the Columbus Story as a spectacle illusion with eyewitness accounts and thereby recover what has become camouflaged and remanufactured. This is done by recovering local ways of knowing, rescuing unknown micro-histories and declaring an obdurate pre-existing social reality that actually exists outside the popularized Columbus Story text that is more than an alternative social construction. Local ways of knowing that had been rendered premodern, native or otherwise illegitimate point to discontinuities, contradictions and ruptures in the harmonious Columbus story. This approach to microstoria also calls into question the progress myth of the Columbus Story (see Table 3.1, assumption 6).

Garden of Eden
In the second approach, the Columbus Story of how capitalism first evolved is challenged as a Garden of Eden imitative narrative by reclaiming microstories of slave catching, land-grabbing and other acts of corporate imperialism in the log book of Christopher Columbus. Admiral Columbus invokes a festive 'Garden of Eden' narrative that when retold in the Spanish court will unleash a rush for gold such as the world has never known. He describes the Taino people 'as naked as their mothers bore them, and the women also …. They are very well-built people, with handsome bodies and very fine faces, though their appearance is marred somewhat by very broad heads and foreheads, more so than I have ever seen in any other race' (Fuson, 1987: 76). This story begins in log entries upon arrival to the first islands. For example, writes First Admiral Christopher Columbus, the first ethnographer of the so-called 'New World', in his ship's log:

> FRIDAY, 12 OCTOBER 1492 At dawn we saw naked people, and I went ashore in the ship's boat, armed, followed by Martin Alonso Pinzon, captain of the *Pinta*, and his brother, Vincente Yanez Pinzon, captain the *Nina*. I unfurled the royal banner and the captains brought the flags which displayed a large green cross with the letters F and Y at the left and right side of the cross. Over each letter was the appropriate crown of that Sovereign. These flags were carried as a standard on all of the ships. After a prayer of thanksgiving I ordered the captains of the *Pinta* and *Nina*, together with Rodrigo de Escobedo (secretary of the fleet), and Rodrigo Sanchez of Sgovia (comptroller of the fleet) to bear faith and witness that I was taking possession of this island for the King and Queen. I made all the necessary declarations and had these testimonies carefully written down by the secretary. In addition to those named above, the

entire company of the fleet bore witness to this act. To this island I gave the name *San Salvador*, in honor of our Blessed Lord. (Fuson, 1987: 75–6)

The great 'discovery' spectacle was performed with exact ceremonial accoutrement, precise ritual and its story entered appropriately into the logbook. If not, the commercial claims of Admiral Columbus would not be recognized by the remote spectators in Spain, or by competing Euro nation states. Queen Isabella and King Ferdinand would not honour his ten per cent commission on all wealth returned to Europe (by any and every-one) along this new trade route to Asia, or to his children, their children, and so on, in perpetuity unless the spectacle was performed according to the rules.

The second voyage

Admiral Columbus on his second voyage of 17 ships had ten native women kidnapped as sex slaves when the first islands were cited. As an Italian nobleman tells this story (we do not have a telling from the native view), there is, I think, evidence that during the second voyage, before coming to the Hispaniola fort, there was a change in how natives were to be treated henceforth:

> While I was in the boat I captured a very beautiful Carib woman, whom the said Admiral [Columbus] gave to me, and with whom, having taken her into my cabin, she being naked according to their custom, I conceived the desire to take pleasure. I wanted to put my desire into execution but she did not want it and treated me with her fingernails in such a manner that I wished I had never begun. But seeing that (to tell you the end of it all), I took a rope and thrashed her well, for which she raised such unheard of screams that you would not have believed your ears. Finally we came to an agreement in such manner that I can tell you that she seemed to have been brought up in a school of harlots. – Michele de Cuneo, an Italian nobleman and passenger on Columbus's second voyage. (Stolcke, 1992: 55)

From this account, it can be argued that Columbus had little or no inten-tion ever of restraining the consumptive appetite of those on this second voyage and had perhaps changed his mind en route, or even earlier. This is no gift giving exchange. Nor, can it be argued without silliness or blatant ignorance that Admiral Columbus was on a religious or cultural mission to civilize the New World into sex slavery.

In March of 1495, Admiral Columbus set out with a force of 20 combat dogs, 25 horses and 200 soldiers across the Island of Haiti/Santa Domingo (Varner and Varner, 1983). The dogs were assigned to Alonso de Ojeda, who knew warfare from fighting the Moors of Granada. Ojeda yelled, 'sic 'em' 'and the royal attack gods hurled themselves at the Indians' naked bodies, grabbed them by their bellies and throats, threw them to the ground, disemboweled them, and ripped them to pieces.' On 5 May 1494 Columbus finding his 39 men slain and his fort in ruin, 'concluded the time had come to make a display of Castilian arms' (Varner, 1983: 5). Not just a display, but a spectacle, and one enacted many times before in the Canary Islands. 'The Indians fled in surprised terror, pursued by a great dog that bit them and did them much harm; for one dog against the Indians was worth ten men. Columbus then went ashore and took possession of the island in the name of the Spanish sovereigns' (Varner and Varner, 1983: 5).

Third approach: seek the middle ground
There is one final microstoria approach I wish to illustrate that extends from the assumption 10 in Table 3.1: between macro logical-deduction and grounded theory-induction is the abduction method of microstoria analysis. This approach links grand narrative analysis (see Chapter 2) with what we have seen thus far in microstoria analysis. Is there a middle ground between grand narrative and microstoria? Can we attain that middle ground with abduction? I would like to illustrate that macro-narrative uses microstory to makes its case and that microstory is often about resisting a grand narrative.

Instead of shattering the grand narrative with the microstoria approaches recently examined, I will look at the interplay of macro and micro-narrative. The Columbus story is still widely advocated, particularly in the US. At the same time, there are pockets of resistance reclaiming the microhistories we have just reviewed. There continues to be a contest between the great man narratives of Columbus and the microstories of Taino and Carib genocide. And there continues to be an interplay of big capital narratives of free market economy and Marxist big narratives of capital exploitation and proletariat resistance. Microstorians, as argued above, reject the macrohistories of Marx as well as those of the capitalists. The focus is on the microstory. Yet, it is possible to set a middle ground and accomplish an interpenetrating analysis of macro and microstory.

Karl Marx, for example, makes frequent reference to the Columbus story in the microstoria approaches (Boje et al., 2000b). The analogy that Marx makes is that the barbaric methods of capital accumulation in the slave owning and trading of the East and West Indies continue to survive in another form in the industrial model. As Marx puts it, 'the civilized horrors over over-work are grafted on the barbaric horrors of slavery, serfdom, etc.' (1867/1967: 36). I am not saying Marx is a microstorian, only that he did prototypical microstorians' recovery of forgotten and marginalized stories through both quantitative and qualitative study.

In sum, in both Marx's 'The Working Day' (see also Chapter 1 in the same Volume) and the Columbus narrative after Washington Irving's (1828) rendition, there is an excess of work prematurely destroying humanity. In both there is work until dead performativity, but with the dog and lash it happens much quicker than with 16 to 18 hour workdays. In both narratives it appears that capital as Marx puts it 'cares nothing for the length of life of labor-power' (1867/1967: 265).

The parallel that Marx draws is that the early factory system (he calls the 'House of Terror') and the conquests of many nation states were forms of 'flesh-peddling' managed by 'flesh-agents' (1867/1967: 268, 277). Marx ends his chapter as follows: 'laborers must put their heads together, and, as a class, compel the passing of a law, an all-powerful social barrier that shall prevent the very workers from selling, by voluntary contract with capital, themselves and their families into slavery and death' (1867/1967: 302). While the working-day laws and the laws against slavery were passed workers did not continue the struggle. The last footnote of the chapter ends with irony as cited from Engels:

> With suppressed irony, and in very well weighed words, the Factory Inspectors hint that the actual law also frees the capitalist from some of the brutality natural to a man who is a mere embodiment of capital, and that it has given him time for a little 'culture.' 'Formerly the master had no time for anything but money; the servant had no time for anything but labor.' (1867/1967: 302)

Marx poses a counter-narrative to the romantic posture of capitalism. Such counter-narrating has arrived only in the last two decades to challenge the heroic legend of Columbus.

Conclusions

In organization studies, microstories can have many applications. Most organization texts present the narrative of the conquering CEO with the same sense of romanticism as Washington Irving (1828) presented the Columbus narrative. The value of microstoria is to reclaim the stories of the 'little people,' the ones doing the work and making the show happen. And the conquering hero narrative can be renarrated in a more multi-voiced text, one that includes the tragic as well as the heroic. When we write the macrostories into the scene, then there is the interplay of the macro (political, social and economic) and the microstory (the people and their lives). The stories and counter-stories fashion a web of stories, an antenarrative soup out of which the tension between microstory and macrostory lives. It is out of this soup that each generation comes along to revise its collective memory from the initial prenarrative (where no story fit the events) to the first attempts to narrate (what happened?), and to renarrated stories thereafter. In Chapter 4, we look at story networking in narrative analysis.

4

Story network analysis

Most narrative study will involve some type of network analysis, the categorizing of story fragments into narrative maps read as nodes and relationships (links) for abstract model building (see Figure 4.1). An antenarrative analysis is focused on the embedded process of story networking. It is not about mapmaking it is about the living relations.

Granovetter (1973) has a theory of weak and strong social network ties that has implications for story network analysis. The particulars of the relationship matter in the analysis. Further, Granovetter (1985) develops a theory of embeddedness in which economic transactions are 'embedded' in the social, cultural, communication and historical particulars of the networking. Here networking becomes an action where stories are shared, referenced and embedded *in situ*. An embedded approach to networks of stories (or antenarratives) is vastly different from an analyst's narration of a simulation network model or a diagram of thematic taxonomy. In terms of antenarrative, I shall argue that the phenomenon of story networking processes and narrative network model representations radically differ.

Narrative network analysis utilizes visual display that is deadening to storytelling dynamics. But this depends, I think, on how one conceptualizes a story network. 'According to most reviewers, visualization plays an important part in the development of almost every field for science' (Freeman, 1999b). This is particularly true when we combine narrative and social network analysis. Here we will look at both the antenarrative soup of human collective existence and the renderings in narrative theory architecture and models.

Social network analysis is a branch of social and behavioural science that tries to understand the complex architectures that evolve from the many social strong or weak ties any individual, group, organization or society maintains. Story network analysis as an antenarrative approach has three applications:

1. It seeks to understand the complex dynamics of storytelling among people across their social networks (e.g. numbered nodes in Figure 4.1). The model is a map of the storytelling or antenarrated territory.
2. The intertextual aspects of stories (see Chapter 5) can be explored in relations to connective interchange (the links in Figure 4.1). However,

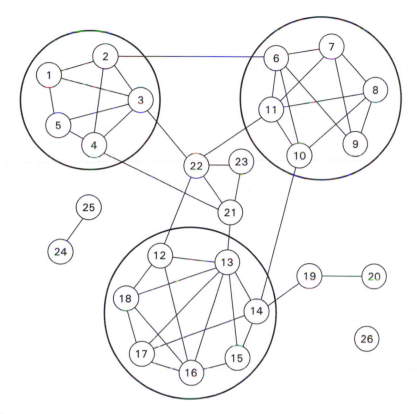

Figure 4.1   *Depiction of story network architecture*

there is a difference between presenting a taxonomic map of how
story themes connect, as seen in the eye of the analyst, and tracing the
patterns of story in the Tamara of the story exchange, *in situ.*

3. A story network analysis can be the basis to set up a virtual complex
    of hyper-links to partially re-enact the interconnectivity of a story net-
    work (this goes beyond the two-dimensional display in Figure 4.1).
    Computer tools can aid in the analysis, display and simulation of net-
    work patterns. The social network focus is on visual and simulation
    mappings of combinations of person, group and/or interorganizational
    story networks.

Story mapping

Story mapping involves displaying social architecture, how one story or
relationship is intertextually linked to another in a sociogram network
display such as in Figure 4.1. A network is a map of nodes and links that
interconnect. Nodes in story network analysis can be people, groups,

organizations, stories, categories, etc. and the links can be analytic or virtual links. Links can depict intensity with various line shadings or symbols (i.e. a frequency or importance rating annotating each link) (see Freeman, 1999a, b, c). A 'node' is a category-container for various ideas, codes, concepts and attributes selected for your analysis. In Chapter 3, for example, we examined how microstorians excavate archival documents from notaries and religious orders to map person-to-person networks, collecting microstories of embedded social ties. But we could just as readily map nodes that are defined as towns, organizations, families or other collectives.

A caution is in order

Network mapping despite its technical modelling and simulation sophistication is a decidedly structuralist approach to narrative analysis. Beyond architecture are all the processes of meaning, historical memory and embedded relationships (Granovetter, 1985). Human processes of meaning construction and embedded social historical dynamics in the construction and transformation of networks can become reified as 'object analysis' in structuralist analysis. Reification is forgetting that a structural object-relation display has subjective meaning and social construction processes beyond the map in the context. The network displays are often simply the analyst's perception of the salient structural features of a storied network, such as its sub-group organization and recurrent narrative themes.

A theory of story network dynamics

Stories are not static; stories web, assemble, disassemble, and otherwise deconstruct one another in self-organizing systems that while being constrained by so-called 'grand' and 'official' narrative are also controlled from the field. That is sanctioned channels and catch points such as scheduled meeting places, briefing times, and managerial speechmaking events and memoranda with deadlines, etc. – constrain, but do not fully control the unfolding story spins. Stories proliferate and people may meet to unravel the interpretations and to disseminate disinformation to distort and deflect meaning. Stories follow these strong ties clusters (i.e. departments, divisions and even organizations), catch points (staging areas for telling and retelling) and weaker ties (more casual meetings across turf boundaries) where story parts jump across a strong ties. Bits and pieces of story traverse weak and strong ties, couple and recouple into alternative tapestries, more complex story assemblages. Unlike the Internet where message 'A' is broken into small chunks that travel alternative pathways and reassemble at some user's terminal, the story network (see Chapter 5) proliferates 'A$^{1'}$', 'A$^{2'}$', 'A$^{3'}$' and 'A$^{4'}$'. There is no 'A' only the cascading assemblage weaving across nets and devouring more bits here and there, into ever-shifting and differing assemblages. We note that the various 'A's' are representations of storytelling activity (again the map is not the territory).

In antenarrative terms, the territory is messier than the map. The versions of stories network and crisscross in ways that allow versions to increase their radical differentiation as in the child's game of telephone (i.e. passing a whispered message from person to person in a line will inevitably result in distortions, deletions, amplifications and strange interpretations). A line is a very limited and simplistic case of story network. In multi-channel, self-organizing networks with many alternative pathways, the story transformation and differentiation process yields geometric displacement at two simultaneous levels. First, the story assemblages differentiate one from another. Secondly, the network itself is constructing new ties, skipping others and weaving unique webs to envelop, sort, broadcast, accommodate and replicate some story assemblages while abandoning others. In this theory of story assemblages and dynamic networking, there never is a 'whole story' or an 'originary story' since even 'eye witnesses' disagree, as do 'historians'. It is in this boiling story assemblage and story disassemblage soup that network analysis commences, as analysts add further assemblages to the concoction. They are never witness to or able to reassemble a 'whole story'.

Story network analysis

Ethnograph, NUD*IST, NVivo and other text analysis software is becoming increasingly popular as structuralist methods to map story themes in qualitative organization studies (Weitzman and Miles, 1995). This search and retrieval software is being used increasingly in story analysis work.

Both NUD*IST and NVivo as well as Ethnograph allow the qualitative researcher to collect a rich array of text fragments from interviews, observations literature and archival review. 'NUD*IST' stands for Non-numerical Unstructured Data Indexing Searching and Theorizing (Qualitative Solutions & Research Pty. Ltd, 1995). 'NVivo' is the partner software-upgrade to NUD*IST (Richards, 1999). My earlier work used Ethnograph (Boje, 1991) to trace story themes in transitions of an office supply firm and NUD*IST (Boje, 1995; Boje et al., 1999) to do a postmodern analysis of Disney stories, but more recently I am using NVivo in order to posit more formally model network relations among stories.

In such analyses, we model types of actor, story, theme, etc. into story network maps. Yet these maps are radically different from the emic networks and story assemblages of organization folk. Parts of folk texts are coded into categories or themes to allow swift access and display in complex network patterns of analyst construction. Mixed in this display are story assemblages that were called forth by the analyst's demand that the folk narrate their experience. Strange documents, comprised of retellings, new tellings and analyst tellings are converted to taxonomies of 'nodes' (ideas, categories, concepts, people, things, etc.). The soup is both more than and less than folk story networks that analysts rip from the field.

The nodes (and entire documents) can be searched and in some instances the links between them can be modelled. Nodes can be shaped into sets or clusters of themes. Node 1 in Figure 4.1 can stand for a single story theme (a label applied to story assemblages) or a cluster of like themes. Alternatively, nodes 1 to 5 can be defined as a cluster of 'strong tie' nodes linked by similar themes.

It is possible using NVivo to construct hypertext 'live' model network displays. On-screen editing of network patterns, nodes, attributes and contexts are also possible. Clicking on a node in a model display can bring up a text, its attributes and relations to classes of other nodes. Again this is both simulation and map of the folk story networking; it is not the terrain. Nodes can be managed in sets and nodes can be coded, linked to other nodes and retrieved in combination for reports and simulation modelling. Models as we shall explore are based upon the ideas and theories of the investigators, who may or may not, develop their maps in close conspiracy with their informants. As modelling gets more sophisticated it will be possible to trace the changing shape or form of analyst networks over time and to embed contextual access to each node (e.g. through hyper-links). NVivo for example allows an analyst to erect different views of a network model (Fraser, 1999: 126). One layer, for example, could be stories relating employees in an official organizational structure (from an organizational chart) while another layer displays stories connecting informal patterns of structure or another layer depicting hegemonic (taken-for-granted) relationships of power and control.

Nodes can be analysed in three ways using NVivo: into tree-like 'hierarchies of nodes', into 'case nodes' such as all workers or all managers, or into 'free nodes' which are unorganized ideas (Richards, 1999: 12–17, 24). As you array nodes into maps, be they hierarchies or some type of Venn diagram, the relevant document bits and pieces are being thrown into new (contrived) contexts of meaning. Colour can also be used to enhance displays (Freeman, 1999c). The visual displays are abstract models of properties thought to relate to the *in situ* context. It may help to think of nodes as 'live links' to contexts, to the 'original' context of collection or enactment rather than 'dead containers' of abstract categories. Or as node-links in hyper-documents where a click takes you from one context to another. 'It is a single living growing tapestry with n dimensions' (Richards, 1999: 24). The uses of such models are limited only by imagination. NVivo allows the computer/software user to include various context views of a coded passage of text (Fraser, 1999: 43). Clicking the mouse on a particular passage will bring up its embedding contextual view.

It has been my experience that the Windows-imitative text processing software is not a replacement for knowing your texts. And it is easy to forget that folkways of networks and analyst network displays differ. In traditional ethnographic work, the task is to build a rapport with the people and analyse the texts as they emerge and transform. The analytic model emerges over time in iterative exchanges, missing and amending stages in the story assemblage process, not as the result of mouse clicks.

The new software may not be such a great improvement. A good set of highlight pens allows the analyst to see more clearly the context of story fragments. The traditional way was to take a transcribed text together with sets of archived documents, field notes and other observations that became texts and, using markers, margin notes, scissors and file folders, begin to organize the data. A log was kept of the emergent coding categories, which are now being referred to as 'nodes' and 'attributes'. As the analysis proceeded the ethnographer shuffled and reorganized notes and folders, combining some, expanding gross codes into more refined catalogues, while keeping the context of in view. As the folder contents took shape, the themes of the study emerged. Gaps could be identified and additional interviewing, participation and observation could focus on filling the empty folders with rich content.

A caveat is that the sophisticated text modelling software is not a substitute for working in the field to find the gaps between analyst maps and folkways and to keep track of the analysis as it unfolds. The danger is that qualitative analysis will turn into SPSS or SAS analysis, where there is a disjuncture between collection and analysis. Even more dangerous is that context could get lost as snippets of text get stored for easy retrieval into electronic databases. However, this said, it is possible to imitate the file folder, multi-coloured marker, margin notes and cut and sort mode with the new qualitative analysis packages. It is easy to get lost in the modelling and forget the narrators.

Some types of story network maps

I will focus on several network mapping variations that relate to stories. The following are five types of story network maps:

1. **Story as links in network maps** – The nodes (e.g. the numbered circles in Figure 4.1) can be names (of people, places or organizations) and the links (lines in Figure 4.1) connect stories among the nodes. The dotted lines are clusters within the network. In Figure 4.1 nodes 1 to 5 form one cluster while 6 to 10 and 12 to 18 form two other clusters, nodes 21 to 23 and 10 to 14 form bridging relations between two or more clusters. Multi-dimensional scaling (MDS) can be used in social network analysis to sort the clusters, minimize distances between highly interactive nodes and identify bridge relations.
2. **Story to context network maps** – Contexts can be nodes in Figure 4.1 and the links are the story lines that connect them. The microstorians trace embedded stories in their historical context without using a contemporary lens or bagging them together in decontextualized collections.

3. **Story as nodes in network maps** – Stories can also be mapped as node clusters (the numbered circles in Figure 4.1) to other story node clusters by their linking themes (lines that associate clusters analytically). Here each node in Figure 4.1 is a story.
4. **Story and time networking** – Stories can be connected in time sequence to other stories, past, present and future. For example S1 could come before S2 and S3 after them both in Figure 4.1.
5. **Story and multi-dimensionality** – There are multi-dimensional mappings of story networks that go beyond the node/line drawing of Figure 4.1. Venn diagrams, for example, can be used that make nodes and lines bigger or smaller, use colour schemes and multiple symbols to depict and map story networks. There are also simulations that do not map so easily into visual coordinates.

I will briefly review each of these five analytic approaches. Visualizations of these interpersonal and interorganizational fields in the examples that follow are presented as a work in progress. The idea is to map the inter-domain ties among storytelling organization systems. In the cases below, this is between Nike, stockholders, consumers, workers, academics and the media. In this way it is possible to visualize and trace inter-system penetration among storytelling domains and relationships.

Stories as links
Story fragments can link to names, such as people, organizations or places. For example, in Chapter 3, the microstorians graphed names in social groups. This was particularly the case for family groups with varying positions in the economic and social strata. Sociograms are a common way to map social networks. Visualization maps of name networks can facilitate new ideas. 'Indeed,' argues Freeman, 'without a graph theoretical foundation it is unlikely that the key concepts in network analysis – concepts like distance, reachability, density, clique, cluster, centrality, betweenness, flow and bridge – would have emerged' (1999a: 1). Clustering algorithms can be used to visually map people, groups, organizations or nations that interact with more frequency closer to each other.

Figure 4.2 is an example of story to name network mapping using studies of Nike to study relations among six storytelling organizations (STOs): Nike Inc., Activists, Media, Workers, Consumers and Studiers. There are other STOs such as government (e.g. President Clinton's No Sweatshop Campaign), other sports wear manufacturers such as Reebok, Puma, Fila, New Balance, etc. which are not part of the present study. The possible links to analyse in Figure 4.2 are numbered 1 to 15. The stories I collected involve several stories to name relationships.

Nike documents, for example, name a number of third party contacts in its website and these include phone numbers of organizational spokespersons. Nike's web documents list some of the most outspoken activists (e.g. Medea Benjamin of Global Exchange and Thuyen Nguyen at Vietnam

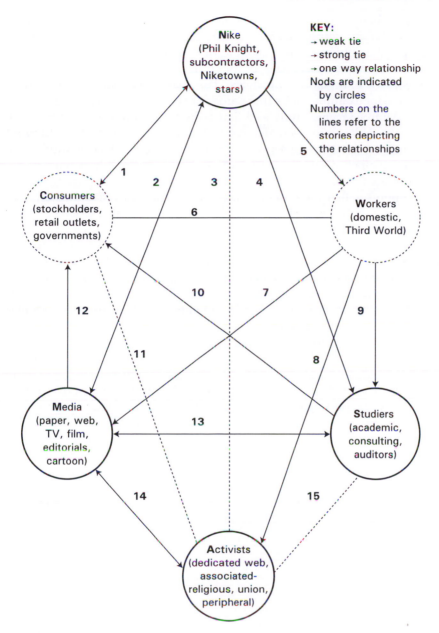

Figure 4.2   *Network of six STOs*

Labor Watch). Nike and activists keep files of press releases, stories and counter-stories on each other on websites. Nike invites consumers and stockholders to call to verify Nike's stories (e.g. the Andrew Young Report name list). One analysis would be to contact the named individuals and get their side of the story. For example, Vidette Mixon, a major shareholder and representative for the Methodist church is on Nike's list. Her speeches and motions at stockholder meetings in 1997 and 1998 have resulted in major concessions by Nike in terms of allowing third party monitors of Nike labour practices. There are other sides to the story. Activists, for example, claim that names are being listed that were not part of the Andrew Young study and that Nike is alleged to engage in disinformation. Nike counters with charges that activists have an axe to grind and that the methodologies of activist studies cannot be trusted. Both accuse the other of spin doctoring which makes story analysis particularly appropriate to this interorganizational field.

The point is that these interactions can be traced to reveal patterns of relationship between nodes (organizations, groups, individuals) and the linking stories. Such an analysis would trace the ways in which the network of multiple storytelling (organizations and groups, i.e. Nike, media, activists, studiers, workers [both domestic and Third World], and consumers [including stockholders and retailers]) circulate and spin stories to influence one another. The point of the analysis could be to say something about the intertextuality of the storytelling network as a whole (see Chapter 5 which gives examples of the interweave of each text).

Each node in Figure 4.2 represents storytellers who claim to have a handle on the truth. Dara O'Rourke, a UN investigator has released a confidential, Nike-contracted, Ernst and Young audit of one of its Vietnam factories to activists and the media. The report differs substantively from what Nike is reporting on its website (Nikeworkers.com) and to its shareholders (Info.Nike.com) at annual meetings. Tracing the impact of this story over time reveals how Nike has had to reform its labour and environmental practices when the report went public. Academic researchers are lined up on both sides of the pro and anti-Nike debates over the Ernst and Young audit implications. This report got the attention of the Corporate Watch people (see Figure 4.2) who are very focused on environmental (worker safety) issues.

Story to context network maps
Stories performed in an *in situ* context have different meanings than stories recreated or invented in an interview (Boje, 1998a). The situation in which each story is performed can be coded and analysed. Narrative passages can be coded and these can be viewed to see their embedded narrative context. In addition, the links from a story can be made to other layers of context, for example, one can look at Nike's side of the story, as well as what the media, academics and activists are saying country by country; or look at how Disney changes its story slightly in Japan, Europe and the US (Boje, 1995).

Story as nodes
Story is intertextual to other stories. One process we can explore in Figure 4.2 is how stories are passed along relational ties as the spin changes

depending upon the audience and the aspects of the story the teller elects to accent. For example, in the pathway (2, 14, 15) Nike can construct a press release to the media (M), which can be spun into a revised story told by activists (A) to studiers (S) who subscribe to a listserv. The activist tale can be combined with worker reports (W) and then released back to the media (M) and become part of news accounts that proceed along one or two-way ties to consumers (12), academics (13) and Nike (2).

In Figure 4.2, for example, there are hundreds of news reports and study reports about workers. A simple story analysis is to compare and contrast stories of Nike's domestic and Third World workers in terms of wages, policies and quality of worklife. Some of the worker stories are union and other activist spokes-pieces for the workers and others are Nike speaking for its workers. Another analysis is to contrast what workers say for themselves and what organizations say workers are saying (i.e. the rebel voice and other side of the story analyses reviewed in Chapter 1). A microstoria focus would get very detailed about particular workers and how they live, who their named relations are at work as well as in their social and family circles.

Story and time networking
Tracing the stories between the named individuals and organizations can reveal moves and counter-moves of the storytelling organizations in Figure 4.2. For example, former Ambassador Andrew Young's reports on labour practices were a response to the highly critical report of Thuyen Nguyen of Vietnam Labor Watch.

The multiple storytelling-interorganizing networks are multi-stranded, embedded and dynamic systems. For example, as a story is released by M or A, N reacts by contracting a counter-story from S, releasing a press release, or pumping up diversionary ad campaigns that can affect C. As N releases new press releases to the media, annual reports to stockholders, ad campaigns to customers, and consultant studies to the academy, the A and M report on N's defensive posturing. Nike, in turn releases stories of A's behaviour in the overall system. The net result is that C, domestic workers, academics, more peripheral M's and A's do not know what to believe. In the main, consumers have to dig deep in the news and the Web to receive a clear account of activists. Academics are divided between those who accept Nike contracts for studies and those who maintain independent and sometimes radical positions. The system is exceedingly complex, as well as dynamic.

The various storytelling organizations each have their own chronology of significant and insignificant events. Obviously, Benjamin Medea is presenting a chronology from one viewpoint while Nike presents a different array from their view. A story analyst can contrast articles and reports to analyse differences in chronologies. There are also books by Katz (*Just Do It*, 1994), Strasser ('Swoosh', 1991) and Jeff Ballinger (*Behind the Swoosh*, 1997) that document differing chronologies. From a microstoria epistemology these differences can be empirically sorted out.

Story and multi-dimensionality

The main types of story relationship depicted are weak ties (3, 6, 11, 15), one-way relations (4, 5, 8, 9, 10, 12) and two-way relations (1, 2, 7, 13, 14). Obviously, each relation can consist of all three types, but for visual clarity and parsimony only the main relation between nodes is displayed. Examples of a weak tie would be Nike's attempt to get a peripheral activist to believe its story or a worker flown over from Indonesia to speak at a rally staged in front of consumers at a store selling Nike products.

Social network mapping can also be used to display hierarchy. Ranking data on the frequency or ranking of stories from the six nodes can be entered into MDS and graphing programs to yield hierarchical analyses. For example, power and resistance involve storytelling prowess. Power in this network is defined here as the ability of a storyteller to get another to abide within and live out the storyteller's plot. Resistance occurs as counter-stories and story spins are constructed and retold along alternate pathways to attempt to change the balance of power relationships. For example, N and the M are assumed to have more power to construct stories of the W. Studiers such as academic social scientists can craft stories of the workers. Workers however can resist N by creating ties to A, S and M because these stories, in turn affect C which can then affect N's reputation and subsequent market share from C. Activists seek to tell stories in ways that get picked up by S and M which can reach M in order to create an impact upon C which will affect N's power over W.

Conclusion

The graphic images of social networks are elegant and intricate but there are limitations. In Chapter 3 the microstorians critiqued the formation of abstract theoretical apparatus that aggregated antenarratives to the point that people and stories were no longer traceable. The multi-dimensional scaling of who is linked to whom are intriguing displays, but may lose the specificity and dynamics of the storytelling system.

In visualizing social storytelling networks it is now possible to use animation and simulation analyses. This may allow us to subordinate the software to a more dynamic analysis. For example, 'Moviemol' (Freeman, 1999a: 8, 1999c: 2) which runs on personal computers can display time-dependent data. Viewers can rotate, translate and zoom in on the moving images. Network images change in the display as the simulation unfolds, possibly revealing patterns that are not easily apparent in a reading of the text. This could allow us to see patterns that are buried in pages of storied texts. The result can even be made into a MPEG movie that can be displayed on web browsers. This could allow us to study the dynamics of the storytelling system, in its simulation, and in the retrieval of filmed episodes.

In sum, story network mapping provides important analytic tools for narrative analysis, but this can cloud the dynamics of antenarrative behaviour. This, however, need not be an either/or relationship. A wide array of MDS and graph modelling tools can be adapted to story analysis. Ethnographic analyses that accumulate storied texts can be combined with simulation work to discern complex social network patterns. The basic assumption is that stories have a mutual impact with the relations an individual is embedded within, and on perception of behaviour and social patterns.

In order to explore the dynamics of social networks, stories can reveal the plots that combine characters. The new software allows us to combine the skills of network analysis and narrative inquiry. Storytelling reveals, for example, the contact patterns among organizational members or among organizations. Innovations in the display such as the use of colour, changeable node sizes, the intensity of lines, etc. allow visual maps a great deal of complex information. Such maps go beyond the tired displays in Figures 4.1 and 4.2. And beyond this is the animation potential for simulated networks. Model building is coming to narrative analysis, and with it will come all the drawbacks of structuralist analysis. These include the reductionism of subjective meaning into object display, the denigration of ethnography into software analysis, and the proliferation of mindless studies that dump a lot of text into a processor and pop out images. Yet, it is also possible to combine a rigorous narrative analysis with sound story collection procedures, participant involvement in the model building, etc. with the new software possibilities. In Chapter 5 I will look at intertextuality which, interestingly enough, at one level is the networking of textual fragments within a narrative and the intertextual web of texts beyond.

5

Intertextuality analysis

Intertextuality is antenarrative since instead of a homogeneous narrative, each text is theorized as a network of fragments that refer to still other narrative texts. Here we will briefly explore how the intertextual system and networking theory of the novel can be extended to organizational studies. I assume each organizational narrative is intertextually related with many others. At the simplest level this is merely dialoguing with and quoting prior texts and anticipating subsequent re-reading and re-citation in many other texts. Each day organizations add more texts to an intertextual world. Each organizational text opens different lines of interrelatedness to preceding and anticipated texts. And each line of utterance in a textual system opens up dialogue with texts of other times and places. As such, the intertextual network is antenarrative in its dynamic, unfinished and embedded qualities.

For definition, I assume 'textual systems' antenarratives are not closed narrative systems, easily compared to other texts along structural functionalist inductive-deductive metrics, but are instead complex, plural and contextualized systems of signifiers suspended in changeable chains of signifiers. There is no whole narrative to taxonomically contrast with another whole text; as such intertextuality is antenarrative.

Intertextuality is not simply a citation index. Intertextuality 'has been generally misunderstood … it has nothing to do with matters of influence by one writer upon another, or with sources of a literary work; it does on the other hand, involve the components of a *textual system* such as the novel, for instance' (Roudiez, 1980: 15). Rather, there is a dynamic textual system in play. In this chapter, intertextuality will be explored on two dimensions:

1. the dimension of the heterogeneous stitch and weave of utterances of a text, and
2. the way a text is part of an ongoing dynamic network of production, distribution, and consumption of antenarratives.

As such, we will be extending the antenarrative 'network analysis' from Chapter 4 in important ways. We will do this by looking at antenarrative production, distribution and consumption networks as intertextual. But, we will add to this a focus on carnival to capture the socially embedded aspects of intertextuality. We begin with Kristeva.

Semiotician Julia Kristeva (1980a, b: 36) in an article written in Paris in 1969 builds on Bakhtin's 'translinguistic' and 'interlingistics' to first define 'intertextuality'. Besides Kristeva's pioneering work based in Bakhtin, Barthes (1957, 1977), Derrida (1976), Foucault (1972: 82) and Fairclough (1992: 101–36) have also added much to intertextual analysis. Four intertextuality points spring from the narrative analysis of novels that we seek to apply to organization narrative.

1. **Textual productivity** – Kristeva observes that the novel is a 'productivity' that is 'redistributive' (destructive-constructive), she notes 'it is a permutation of texts, an intertextuality: in the space of a given text, several utterances, taken from other texts, intersect and neutralize one another' (1980a, b: 36–8).
2. **Social and historical intertextual networks** – Besides the juxtaposition of various voices, quotes and narrative interpretations in novels, intertextuality is also the social and historical network that interlaces a novel with other texts. Novels are produced to be distributed and to be consumed, to link past texts with present and anticipated texts.
3. **Intertextual distribution and consumption** – Novels are intertextual in terms of covert struggles for power that is dialogically embedded in its production, distribution and consumption.
4. **Intertextuality and carnival** – There is one final element of the novel that has relevance to organizational narratives – they are carnivalesque spectacles. This last point needs a bit more elaboration before we proceed to demonstrate the analysis.

Carnivalesque narrative intertextual systems

Kristeva says carnival is the double, 'it is a spectacle, but without a stage; a game, but also a daily undertaking; a signifier, but also a signified' (1980b: 78). What is pioneering about Kristeva's work goes unnoticed in contemporary intertextuality analysis: *intertextuality is inter-related with carnival*. When modernity freed itself of monologic author (and god), the carnivalesque was released with the force of the polyphonic novel.

I submit to you that we write about organizational stories and scenes that are increasingly carnivalesque, an intertextual analysis of antenarrative is highly appropriate. Disney, the decadent casino-hotels of Las Vegas, and Nike hyper-media increasingly construct carnivalesque theatrical stages that enrol customers in spectacular interpretations of corporately narrated identity.

For Kristeva 'the scene of the carnival introduces the split speech act: the *actor* and the *crowd* are each in turn simultaneously subject and addressee of discourse' (1980b: 46). The author, dead or not, combines 'carnivalistic play' with its non-discursive logic of binary oppositions (i.e. good/evil, hero/villain, rich/poor, male/female, actor/spectator) that his/her narrating will necessarily, obligingly or be forbidden to resolve

(Kristeva, 1980b: 44). And for institutions the theatrical resolve is to render various class, race, gender distinctions harmonious and therefore hegemonic with the 'common sense' legitimation of corporate texts, including strategy, identity and harmonious rationales for labour and ecological practices.

Each intertextual system is constituted within carnivalesque spectacle performative of which the corporate authoring of textual or narrative accounts is only one participant. Several sign systems compete for representational authority, to sell one way of interpreting otherwise polyphonic subject positions, including legitimating labour practices and idea struggles.

Intertextual analysis is misunderstood when we miss the important carnivalesque ways analysts have gone beyond comparative, functionalist or structuralist protocols to the exploration of a polyphonic intertextual system that recontextualizes the power struggle.

Carnival within intertextual production, distribution and consumption

In intertextual analysis we look for a crowd of authors, actors and readers engaged in carnivalesque scenes of dynamic textual production, distribution and consumption. Spectacles are enacted to be read as texts along corporately controlled points of view. Intertextuality therefore violates the context-free assumptions of monologic comparative and structuralist analyses since it does not stop with a status quo reading of power. Context-free comparative analysis assumes a live authoritative author, a totalized bounded text, and an impartial observer/reader standing outside that text to read universalized meaning. In analysing the intertextual weave, the hegemonic aspects of 'ready made' textual interpretations for distribution and consumption become more apparent (Fairclough, 1992).

From a postmodern position, I must reflect upon my own construction of intertextual analysis, where I am choosing particular authors, quotations and examples to design a ready-to-hand 'critical' reading of the perversions of corporate power. This author is not 'dead'. It is no accident that Barthes (1977) follows his 'introduction to the Structural Analysis of Narratives' with two of his most famous essays 'The Death of the Author' and 'From Work to Text'. His use of intertextuality asserts that the mere act of observing a text changes the text. As Kristeva puts it, the author is '(author + spectator)' and very much a part of the carnival scene, part of acts of production, distribution and consumption. And I too am part of a history of intertextual scenes. While the author is dead, the citations, tables and quotes attributed to others that get bound together by narrative, as in this chapter, unveil for Kristeva (1980a: 45–6) a writer and at times an institution, even a publisher and an academy as principal actors in the speech play that ensues in the intertextual system.

Global social contexts

➢ Whose social identities get constituted? ➢ Who has access to being included in the text? ➢ Who does the text quote? ➢ Who speaks for whom? ➢ What institutions commission the text?	➢ Whose conventions (genres, styles and types) does the text incorporate? ➢ Who is the text distributed to for consumption? ➢ Who are the audiences this text is designed to be interpreted and read by?
➢ How are parts of other texts incorporated into the text (quoted or interpreted)? ➢ How are various stories incorporated? ➢ What is the time and place of each utterance? ➢ Where are the footprints of the author?	➢ What is selected as newsworthy for target audiences? ➢ What are the 'common sense' or 'insider' terms? ➢ What are the parodies, ironies and metaphorization? ➢ What interpretative matrix does the author construct for readers to consume?

Precedent texts (left) | *Anticipated texts* (right)

Local contexts

Figure 5.1   *Historicity and social questions for intertextual analysis*

Kristeva argues that each text has an intertextual 'trajectory' of both 'historical' and 'social coordinates' (1980a: 36). For Fairclough (1992) it is a trajectory that is embedded in hegemonic struggle, in selling ways of making sense; distributing those ways for mass consumption. And, therefore, I too am selling a way of making sense for mass training of qualitative analysts of corporate texts. Textual analysis is no longer univocal, texts are interweaves and permutations of many voices, conventions (protocols for social science narrative, including citation and interpretation) and audiences (as in the crowd at carnival). They are intertextual in composition and in their positions in distribution and consumption networks (i.e. corporate text analysis courses), as well as in chains of power (editors, publishers, media that own publishers, accrediting bodies, designers of curriculum, science wars).

Figure 5.1 depicts the horizontal dimension of the historicity of the texts that precede and are anticipated in an intertextual system, and a vertical dimension of its immediate and distant contexts. As Kristeva (1980b: 65) argues the text is a social and cultural activity but, as Fairclough (1992: 91–6) reminds us, also a hegemonic one. These are the authors I cite to legitimate my own construction of intertextual analysis which I can only anticipate will be distributed and consumed.

When I compare and contrast the structure or function of texts, one to another, I mask the dynamic, moving generation of power structures in relation to changing social and historical contexts and networks of distribution and consumption presented in Figure 5.1.

For Kristeva (1980b: 65), it was Bakhtin's dialogic of text and context and his concepts of the polyphonic and carnivalesque novels that demarcated intertextual from structural or comparative analyses. As Barthes put it, 'the text is plural' (1977: 159). Antenarrative is plural in the social identities that get constituted, access to inclusion, the voices that get included, the audiences that stories are designed to be read by, the conventions of style that get incorporated in corporate acts of writing, and the ambivalence of interpretation in multiple sign systems. Since the antenarrative is plural, the danger to corporate power and managerialist control is that different readers will interpret it quite differently. The hegemonic task of corporate discourse is therefore to yield readings that are harmonious and consistent with strategic local and global practices. My analytic task, as a critical postmodernist is to pierce the veil of reading narratives from the top, without including the microstoria (see Chapter 3).

While for Barthes an intertextual analysis could begin with the observation that the text is woven with 'citations, references, echoes, cultural languages' he does not stop there (1977: 160). For there is a whole historicity, productivity and genealogy that make each antenarrative an intertextual system. Indeed Foucault asserts 'there can be no statement that in one way or another does not reactualize others' (1972: 92). And each antenarrative is 'plural', a 'weave of signifiers' in an ongoing weaving and interweaving fabric of precedent and anticipated texts. As such each storytelling system has a genealogy, as Foucault has explored in the history of 'madness', the 'clinic' and the 'prison'. Therefore the meaning of the signifying intertextual systems is dynamic. Each story is part of an ongoing dialogue with local and more societal, even global contours that rearticulates meaning in embedded acts of retrospective sensemaking.

Barthes 'renders illusionary [an] inductive-deductive science of texts':

> The intertextuals in which text is held, it itself being the text-between of another text, [intertextual] is not to be confused with some origin of the text: to try to find the 'sources,' the 'influences' of a work is to fall in with the myth of filiation; the citations which go to make up a text are anonymous, untraceable, and yet *already read*: they are quotations without inverted commas. (1977: 160)

This to me is an antenarrative theory, a sense that in the storied soup there is no origin, no totalized story, and only temporary agreement, here and there.

It is not the citations and incorporations themselves, but how they are interwoven in three phases of intertextual analysis we will explore. First, the phase of producing an intertextual system of quotes and interpretations.

Secondly, the phase of how antenarrative utterances are distributed in space and time. And thirdly, how the antenarrative presents interpretations as common sense utterances, ready to be consumed in matrices of inter-pretation that contextualize a fashionable meaning. And, as a dynamic, complex and plural *antenarrative system* there are no fixed and static points of meaning for de-contextualized inductive-deductive comparison. Rather the antenarratives have both an historical and a social dialogic enunciation (Kristeva, 1980b: 77). And it is their polysemy dynamism that makes intertextuality misused when done in the static analysis of narra-tive methodology.

Certainly organization antenarratives are not static or stable, but always dynamic, polysemous, dialogic and historical intertextual webs. Organization antenarratives historically elaborate and socially produce themselves in relation to other texts and intertexts, and do so in functional and structural static masks that veil their more carnivalesque logic. And it is the carnivalesque spectacle and theatrics of antenarrative production and ongoing revision that intertextuality can explore. Storytelling systems are also ideological and hegemonic.

To be hegemonic is to exercise power without notice in the taken-for-granted subterrain of socialization and preparing stories that are ready to hand over to consumptive appetites. Organizations, for example, pro-duce press releases to be distributed and consumed 'harmoniously' as 'common sense' accounts that are designed to be 'taken-for-granted' nar-ratives that do not mobilize resistance or bring any attention to ongoing power struggles over institutional sensemaking. In short, hegemonic power operates behind the scenes in acts of socialization, in providing frames that make one's action appear harmonious and neutral.

My point is simple: one errs in looking at intertextual analysis as an exploration of narrative referentiality, such as in the hyper-link text with-out also looking to the carnivalesque. It is more an issue of looking beyond the border of the static text, to its social and historical contextual intertextuality, to its antenarrative systematics in ongoing dialogue, sensemaking and spectacle.

An example of intertextual analysis: nike press releases

To make this distinction clear, I will analyse a simple text, a Yahoo News item posted Thursday 24 September 1998 at 1:24 AM EDT (I have added numbers at the end of each sentence). Yahoo is reprinting an Associated Press release (Nike Shareholders, 1998). I will apply several questions from Figure 5.1 to the intertextual analysis.

Associated press (AP) release

Nike shareholders nix pay proposal

MEMPHIS, Tenn. (AP) – Nike Inc. shareholders on Wednesday rejected a proposal to tie executive compensation more closely to the wages that are paid at the company's contract factories in Asia [1].

Chairman Phil Knight, who made $1.7 million in salary alone last year, promised more improvements and independent monitoring of conditions at its Asian factories, where some workers make $20 [per] month [2].

Shareholder John Harrington had asked Nike to boost its wages in Asia to improve the shoe giant's image and maintain its stock value [3].

'Across the United States these days there are a lot of children who are not looking on Nike in a favorable fashion,' said Harrington, a California investment manager [4].

Harrington introduced the proposal on behalf of Jeanne Henry, a Portland, Ore., shareholder who last year told Knight that her 12-year-old daughter was boycotting the company because of its labor practices at contractor factories in southeast Asia [5].

Nike has been repeatedly criticized for the low wages and working conditions in its Asian factories, which the company has taken steps to improve [6].

Nike spokeswoman Maria Eitel, hired nine months ago as Nike's vice president for corporate responsibility, said the company's Asian factories have successfully implemented a new age minimum of 18 [7]. By the end of the year, the Asian factories will meet US air quality standards [8].

'Make no mistake about it, we'll challenge inaccurate information,' Eitel said [9]. 'But we're not afraid to take criticism. We will listen and we will do something about it.' [10]

Harrington said that Knight earned 5,273 times the annual pay of the average worker in Nike shoe factories last year [11]. Average executive pay in Japan is about 16 times the average worker's, and in Germany it's about 21 times as large, he said [12].

The shareholder proposal calls for Nike to more closely link executive pay to financial performance. It notes that the company already links pay to performance, and that Nike has constantly improved labor practices [13].

Nike will announce soon another pay raise for its Indonesian workers, after the 15 percent raise mandated by Indonesian authorities last spring, Eitel said [14].

Also during the meeting, Knight dismissed reports that Nike was de-emphasizing its 'swoosh' trademark and 'Just Do It' slogan to reduce visibility at a time when Nike has been heavily criticized for its Asian labor practices [15].

'Elimination of either one is either suicidal or crazy and we're not that bad,' Knight said [16].

The swoosh, however, was virtually unseen during Wednesday's meeting [17].

Intertextual analysis of production   We can look at the social relations of the press release's intertextual system production, the heterogeneity of texts that are being woven together. The production begins in the spectacle performances of the shareholders' meeting that are enacted as material utterances for incorporation into reporters' notes. The scene is a Nike shareholders' meeting, a site of corporate production of its own spectacle and the attempts to sell valuations and interpretations of corporate identity that ensue in reporter write-ups. Nike shareholders' meetings have become increasingly carnivalesque, as sites of turmoil, demonstration and contest over issues of narrative meaning, monitoring and changing Asian employee wage, health and safety practices.

Members of the press and activists assemble along with shareholders and executives and staff to hear speeches, short stories, praises and curses, including cameo appearances of sports and corporate celebrities. The AP is one among many, including corporate writers, who will produce releases to the press (see Nike's press release, p. 83 below). The crowd gathers to collectively perform acts of narrative and theatrics that will be renarrated, reinterpreted and distributed for mass consumption through many official, invited and uninvited press releases. Shareholders' meetings are not just times to report the progress of business activities, but carnival time, spectacles enacted and produced to generate press releases to many audiences with many interests.

In terms of narrative production, we can ask the following: who gets quoted? Who gets summarized? Where are the interpretations? Whose voice makes up each utterance in the AP text? Who gets invited to perform? Who edits? The AP press release is a permutation and synthesized utterance of several texts. In terms of narrative inclusion, there are direct quotes from John Harrington, a California investment manager, Maria Eitel, a Nike spokeswoman, and Nike Chairman Phil Knight. While outside, an anonymous voice of a writer, perhaps many writers and several editors, is prominent. We will look at each voice in the release.

The directly quoted texts (Harrington, Eitel and Knight) form one sign system (textual fragments) that is juxtaposed with the writers' sign system of interpretative utterances. This is the definition of Bakhtin's dialogism, a doubling of another logic system that produces intertextual dialogue. It is double in at least two ways. First, the author's logic system doubles with the (selected) speakers' who are being quoted or summarized. Secondly, the writer is deviating from the chronological (causal and linear) sequence of spectacle utterances to constitute a narrative time. Narrative time is being crafted by taking some speakers, certain comments, and setting them out in narrative sequence along side interpretative utterances. And in this way the speakers' (performers') words are subordinated to the writer's words (in number and comprehension). The writer therefore has control over the signification of the utterance by the way the piece has been sculpted. As Kristeva puts it, the writer 'uses another's words, giving it a new meaning while retaining the meaning it already had' (1980b: 73).

The writer is an 'author/actor' constructing his/her voice in dialogic response to others in the design of the release (1980b: 45). Juncture and translative devices are used to stitch the quotes and writer's narrative commentary together, for example, 'Nike Inc. shareholders on Wednesday rejected' (1) and the title, 'Nike Shareholders Nix Pay Proposal'. These and other dialogic moves construct a double signification and render the text ambivalent (polylogical), a joining of two sign systems giving primacy to his/her own commentary. Compare these quotes and interpretations with the official Nike press release. These press releases produce and construct two different totalizing themes out of the fragments of citations (quotes) and writer-narratives. The most important point here is that the symbolic relationships in narrative time take precedence over the substance and causality of chronological time in both releases. These press releases, like all press releases (but also scientific write-ups and ethnographies), transgress the bounds of 'realistic description' to become dialogic moves of production and double signification within and between textual systems.

The author (or authors and editors) of the AP as well as the Nike press release is not provided. There is no 'I' voice or by-line to be attributed to the writer. AP and Nike writers are frequently (not always) coded into press releases as anonymous, non-persons, as witnesses without any acknowledged identity. AP and the Nike Corporation both have reputations for reporting objectively, quoting accurately telling the story as eyewitnesses and giving dependable historical accounts to various audiences. Yet we know someone wrote each release, was present at the event to ask questions and made notes and tape recordings of the speeches. In each case corporate officials made editorial decisions. We also know each press release reporter is more than a copier, transcriber or mechanical recorder of the shareholder meeting, because if we cross out all the sentences with quotation marks (see sentences 4, 9, 10 and 16 in the case of the AP press release), there are still 12 utterances written by someone. Further, the writers exercised their anonymous freedom to include some speakers' comments, summarize others and ignore most altogether. Thus, the writer is a character in the polyphonic intertextual production, one with an interpretive point of view, and more importantly the moderator and gatekeeper of the dialogue. Besides the writer, several other characters appear and are quoted, summarized or represented in each text.

The first character to be quoted in the AP press release is Harrington. Harrington's utterances are revealed in several stages. The writers lead into Harrington's remarks with facts about Knight's and Asian factory workers' salaries (2), and follow with the writer's summary of what Harrington asked (3). In both sentences it is not Harrington who is speaking but the writer of the release. Secondly, there is an utterance of Harrington in quotation marks (4). An investment manager is stating the opinion of a 'lot of children' who can see Nike is no longer 'favorable fashion'. Finally, sentence 5 sets out the story of the mother and 12-year-old daughter who Harrington represents and gives an explanation why the little girl would be protesting, but noting that the 'company has taken steps to improve' (6). The press release thereby stories a conflict between a 12-year-old girl and Nike Chairman Phil Knight. Harrington speaks 'on behalf of Jeanne Henry' a shareholder who speaks for 'her 12-year old daughter', who was 'boycotting the company because of its labor practices at contractor factories in southeast Asia' (see 5). This is more than a conflict between the 12-year-old girl, her mother, an investment manager and the Nike Corporation; it is also a story of differences in Asian workers and CEO salaries and differences over what is a living wage between various boycott groups and Nike, as besides raises, there have been payacts. The 12-year-old girl symbolizes the struggle of Nike and the Nike boycott groups as well as divisiveness over what image Nike should be portraying to maintain stock prices and loyalty (1). In sum, the writer is author and spectator, both a witness to the events and a commentator/participant/actor.

The utterances of Harrington are spliced in such a way as to connote aggressivity towards Nike's policies and to send a message to Nike's management, fellow shareholders and the media. The writer cannot be an objective witness and chronicler of the meeting since s/he is translating and configuring the representation and meaning of the dialogue. It remains an ambivalent intertextual system, designed to be read differently by different audiences.

Nike press release

Nike holds annual meeting in Memphis
– Company Salutes Athletes for Community Involvement –

Beaverton, Ore. (Sept. 23, 1998) – Nike, Inc., the world's leading producer of sports and fitness apparel and footwear, conducted its annual shareholders meeting today in Memphis, Tennessee, site of the company's second largest employee population outside of its home state of Oregon [1].

'If Oregon is Michael Jordan to Nike, Memphis is Scottie Pippen – a model of teamwork; understanding each other's roles and winning championships year in and year out,' Nike founder and chief executive officer Philip H. Knight told shareholders and employees at the Orpheum Theater in downtown Memphis [2].

Nike officials said the shareholders meeting was being held in Memphis to salute its employees there and the city of Memphis, allowing Nike to give something back to a community that has contributed greatly to its past growth and will play an important role in its future success [3].

Nike opened its Tennessee operations in 1983, where it now employs 1,731 workers who distribute its footwear and apparel to retail stores around the United States [4]. Its two distribution centers (DC) have a total of 1,285,600 square feet. Last year, Nike opened a $21.5 million expansion to its apparel DC, adding about 400 new jobs in the past two years. In fiscal year 1998, Nike paid $48.3 million in payroll in Tennessee; $7 million in state and local taxes; $54 million to local Tennessee companies (suppliers); and donated $1 million in cash and products to Memphis charities [5].

During the meeting, Knight and company president and chief operating officer Thomas E. Clarke reported on Nike's business during the last fiscal year. In addition, Larry Miller, president of the Jordan Brand, presented his plans for that new business. Maria Eitel, vice president of corporate responsibility, reported on Nike's efforts related to the environment, community involvement, and worker health and safety [6].

Eitel then introduced two of Nike's athlete-partners: WNBA star Jamila Wideman of the Los Angeles Sparks and San Antonio Spur all-star center David Robinson. Wideman was chosen by USA Today this week for its 1998 Most Caring Athlete Award for her 'hoopin' with Jamila' program, which combines basketball skills clinics with a reading and writing program for under-served young women ages 10–18 [7].

Robinson is well-known for his community service, particularly in San Antonio, Texas [8]. Last week it was announced that the seven-time NBA All-Star is committing – through the David Robinson Foundation – $5 million toward the establishment of The Carver Complex in San Antonio [9]. The complex, which will cover three city blocks, will include a college preparatory school, a civic center and a performing arts venue, and will provide a variety of social, economic and cultural services [10]. The mission of the David Robinson Foundation is to support programs which address the physical and spiritual needs of the family [11]. In conjunction with the Spurs, Robinson established Mister Robinson's Neighborhood, a seven-year old program encouraging students to stay in school and remain drug-free [12].

'There's been a lot of negative focus this year on how much professional athletes are paid, or on a few who have had personal problems, but there is a lot of good news, too,' said Eitel [13]. 'Athletes from Jamila and David to Michael Jordan, Jackie Joyner-Kersee, Mark McGwire, Andre Agassi, Cynthia Cooper and Tiger Woods and so many others are not only heroes on the athletic field, but they're also doing a world of good in our communities' [14].

Earlier in the week, Memphis' own Penny Hardaway of the Orlando Magic joined Memphis Mayor WW Herenton, children served by the Goodwill Boys & Girls Club, Cummings Elementary School principal Robert Terrell and Nike officials to dedicate a basketball court newly refurbished by Nike [15]. The new court surface is made from the soles of recycled athletic shoes [16]. In addition, Hardaway donated $25,000 from the sale of his (and Li'l Penny's) book, *Knee High and Livin' Large*, which Nike matched for a total of $50,000 to identify and train Memphis-area college students to coach youth leagues through Nike's P.L.A.Y. Corps program [17]. Nike also will fund a full-time coach at the site to provide programming for children this coming year [18].

On Tuesday night, Nike's board of directors hosted a private reception for community leaders at the National Civil Rights Museum in Memphis [19]. Among the athletes in attendance were David Robinson, Jamilla Wideman, Penny Hardaway, Cedric Henderson of the Cleveland Cavaliers and Lorenzen Wright of the LA Clippers [20].

In the US, Nike employs 11,759 workers, 1,100 of whom are involved in manufacturing [21]. The company estimates that more than 74,000 people are indirectly employed in retail jobs as the sale of Nike products in this country [22]. Fifty-three percent of the apparel Nike sells in the US is made in this country by an additional 5,400 garment full-time factory workers, and 847 materials mills factory workers [23]. Nike donated $34 million in cash and products to charities globally last year [24].

Nike Inc., based in Beaverton, Oregon, creates authentic athletic footwear, apparel, equipment and accessories for sports and fitness enthusiasts [25]. Wholly owned Nike subsidiaries include Cole Haan, which designs and sells a line of high-quality men's and women's dress and casual shoes and accessories; Sports Specialties Corporation, which markets licensed headwear; and Bauer, Inc., which designs, markets and sells Bauer and Nike hockey equipment, including ice and roller hockey skates, protective gear, sticks and in-line skates [26].

In the Nike press release, the first quoted character is Phil Knight, with utterances and a metaphoric comparison of Jordan/Oregon and

Pippen/Memphis abstracted from his performance on the stage of the Orpheum Theater (see 2). This is followed with an indirect quote of what 'Nike officials' said is the reason for coming to Memphis instead of the traditional site of the shareholders' meetings in Oregon (see 3). Note these two lines along with the citations of Nike investments in Tennessee produce an interpretation as to why Nike is in Memphis instead of Portland for its annual meeting. Line 6 lists corporate officials who spoke at the meeting (Knight, Clarke, Miller and Eitel). According to Nike's press release 'Nike officials said the shareholders meeting was being held in Memphis to salute its employees there and the city of Memphis, allowing Nike to give something back to a community that has contributed greatly to its past growth and will play an important role in its future success' (Nike press release, 1998). As other sources report, 'Nike has moved its annual stockholders meeting this year far away from its hometown of Portland, Oregon to Memphis. In recent years, protesters have protested outside the stockholder meetings and those with passes have asked pointed questions inside, much to the embarrassment of Nike management' (CLR, 1998). And in 1999, the shareholders' meeting was moved further away from Beaverton, Oregon to the Netherlands. What is not reported in the AP press release is interesting. While the shareholders voted down tying Knight's salary to employee wage levels in Asia, Nike announced on 14 August that Phil Knight was not awarded an annual bonus for the recent fiscal year, 'cutting his pay to $1.68 million.... Knight, including his family and charitable trust, holds a 34 percent stake in Nike' (*Bloomberg News*, 14 August 1998).

Line 7 in the Nike press release indicates Eitel introduced sports stars, Wideman and Robinson whose performances set up Eitel's quote in line 13. This is the only other direct quote in the press release which is an example of metadiscourse, a comment on the discourse about 'how much professional athletes are paid' and their 'personal problems'. I interpret the quote as an ideological control over other possible interpretations of wage disparity being produced, such as in the case of the AP press release. Comparing the themes of the two releases reveals that the AP press release produces a signification theme different from Nike's by framing the duality (disparity) between executive and Asian employee wages in place of the one framed by Nike between sports celebrity and Asian employee wages. Also in the Nike press release the 'employee population' (1, 4, 21, 23) is limited to the US population of employees, while in the AP release the population of Nike employees includes half a million Asian employees (see 1, 2, 3, 5, 11 and 14).

Intertextual analysis of distribution   Intertext is released into a distributive system. Each release is a dialogic response to past press releases, media articles and to anticipated releases and articles that may incorporate quotes and interpretations from each release. Each release is a link in a never-ending chain of releases that will become part of news columns, instructor and student notes and college textbooks, including this one. Besides who gets quoted, there is a question of 'what gets situated as newsworthy and analysis-worthy by various writers for target audiences in each chain?'. Eitel (as well as Knight), for example, is quoted in both press releases. In the AP release we are told she was hired 'nine months ago', an item that we can interpret as newsworthy, but also a dialogic response to a prior release (i.e. the news of her hiring and the various interpretations or signification of such a corporate event to investors, consumers, faculty and students of organizational behaviour and strategy). And her hiring is an intertextual event with its own social, even global, context. Eitel's hiring is not the subject *per se* of Nike's press release, but it is about what Eitel does at Nike, who she introduced at the Orpheum Theater and how she interprets Nike's bad news (i.e. 14). However, both releases are part of a wider array of press releases, media articles and commentaries on the signification of Eitel's hiring, including laudatory and critical reviews of her narrative performances.

Binole, for example, writes: 'Her hiring comes in the wake of worldwide battering of the athletic shoe and apparel manufacturer for its foreign labor practices and a decline in domestic footwear sales' (1998a: 1). And she has had 'stints with President George Bush, Microsoft Corp. in Europe and the publicly-supported National Public Broadcasting' (Binole, 1998a: 1). An original Nike press release of her hiring tries to anchor 'one meaning' among many possible meanings, and quotes Thomas E. Clarke as saying: 'Maria's arrival signals Nike's commitment from the top to be a leader not only in developing innovative footwear, apparel and equipment, but in global corporate citizenship' (Nike press release, 1998a). Also in terms of anticipated history, 'Eitel, 35, expects to sit in on senior management meetings and reports directly to Nike chairman Phil Knight and president Thomas Clarke. She will be in charge of about 50 people working in three areas: environmental issues, community involvement and labor relations' (Binole, 1998a: 1).

Each press release enters an intertextual distribution system of many press releases, each with a different interpretative schema. The *Wall Street Journal*, for example, in reporting Eitel's hiring put a spin on it that is thematically similar to AP's press release:

> Nike has been blasted by critics in the last few years, because the company employs questionable employee relations practices. To diffuse that criticism, they have hired a public relations expert to oversee their employment practices. The new executive Maria Eitel, was hired from, of all places, Microsoft. (1998: B14)

Other media reports give Eitel positive reviews. Manning, for example, a reporter for the Oregonian press, stated 'In contrast to its embattled defiance of the past, Nike under Eitel has admitted that some problems existed in the factories and made improving relations with the company's vocal critics a top priority' (1999). The distribution system also has more polemic, even judgmental writers. Hightower (1998) for example contends, 'The giant shoemaker, a notorious sweatshop exploiter, announced that she'll now be responsible for shaping-up Nike's labor practices. Company president Thomas Clarke declared that the hiring of Ms. Eitel "signals Nike's commitment from the top to be a leader ... in global corporate citizenship"' (1998). Hightower closes with a metaphorization that resituates the Nike press release he is parodying: 'Nike's new "VP for Corporate Responsibility" is just another public relations cover-up. This is Jim Hightower saying ... they can put French perfume on a skunk, but it still won't hide the stink' (1998) (see also Hazen, 1998).

Besides Eitel, Phil Knight is also quoted in both releases. In the AP release, 'Elimination of either one is either suicidal or crazy and we're not that bad' (16). The AP authors also drop quotation protocol and just speak for Knight:

'Also during the meeting, Knight dismissed reports that Nike was de-emphasizing its "swoosh" trademark and "Just Do It" slogan to reduce visibility at a time when Nike has been heavily criticized for its Asian labor practices [15].' There is a social and historical context here with regards to 'reports' about the 'swoosh' logo and 'Just Do It' slogan. In 1988 Dan Wieden designed the 'Just Do It' Campaign for Nike, but in January 1998, Nike switched to the 'I Can' slogan. Manning (1997), for example, reports 'Like "Just Do It," the new "I Can" tagline was created by a Portland advertising agency, Wieden and Kennedy'; 'The company takes a risk calculated to boost sales despite fickle fashion trends and sullied sports appeal' and 'Nike Inc. is benching its venerable advertising slogan in hopes of reversing downward sales trends and addressing troubling image issues that plagued the Beaverton company during 1997.'

The 1997 AP press release has an arbitrary ending. When the *Sun News* reported the AP press release, it ended with 'Nike will announce soon another pay raise for its Indonesian workers, after the 15 percent raise mandated by Indonesian authorities last spring, Eitel said'. It left off the item about 'Just Do It.'

Manning adds his own commentary, 'The phrase so rich in youthful attitude became a liability at times in the ongoing debate over conditions in the Asian factories where Nike products are made.' Note, in Nike's press release the image problems are those of the sports celebrities rather than Nike practices. In activist press releases and websites, critics have resituated the Nike slogan with 'Just-ice Do It' 'Just Don't Do It' and the swoosh has been redrawn with a drop of blood from its mouth and as the swooshtika, and in combinations 'Just Say No to the Swoosh.' The 'I Can' campaign has had its own parodies. As Binole reports the 'I Can' advertising campaign has been smitten with similar re-imaginings:

NBC's promos for 'Working' had characters from the show proudly proclaiming what they could do. 'I can file my nails.' 'I can lean way back in my chair without falling – sometimes.' The ads made their debut during Super Bowl Sunday.

'Shortly after they first aired, the people from Nike called our people, and it was a very cordial conversation,' said Pat Schultz, an NBC spokeswoman. 'They said, "Look, we admire your creativity, but we're trying to launch this new campaign, and it's a serious campaign. It's so early on, maybe you could run them later."' (1998b)

Baum's interpretative frame integrates and bridges interpretative themes that we see manifest in both releases:

And professional sports – at the heart of much of Nike's marketing – has been shaken by bad publicity this year from such incidents as Mike Tyson's ear-biting and Latrell Sprewell's assault on his coach. Also, Nike has been criticized for poor working conditions in factories run by overseas subcontractors that produce Nike products. (1997)

Outside these quotations in the AP press release, there are also anonymous utterances by the omniscient narrator, perhaps borrowed or plagiarized from other texts, such as the statement 'Chairman Phil Knight, who made $1.7 million in salary alone last year, promised more improvements and independent monitoring of conditions at its Asian factories, where some workers make $20 month.' The statement reads like it comes from the notations of a reporter on the spot, but we do not know how the utterances were produced, anymore than the statistics and quotations in the Nike press release. We do not know if this is a reference to a company press release, or to Phil Knight's presentation at this shareholders' meeting on 21 September 1998, or to the well-publicized (12 May 1998) National Press Club luncheon announcement of new Nike initiatives to further improve factory working conditions worldwide. The point is there is a plurality of voices, persons, organizations and places that makes up the social fabric of the press release.

Intertextual analysis of consumption   Intertexts are produced to be distributed in intertextual systems and to be consumed by anticipated audience schemata (viewpoints of readers and also writers of subsequent texts). There is a historicity we can analyse by asking what is this text's relation to texts that precede and follow it as well as the genealogy of the interpretative schemata. The press release becomes an utterance in the carnivalesque drama and spectacle of which the writers of both press releases are witness and participant. The AP release was reproduced in other outlets, such as *The Sun Morning News* of Pittsburgh, Kansas (27 September 1998), but in this case the title was changed to 'Nike shareholders reject wage proposal'.

From the title of the AP release, the end of the narrative is already known and it is reaffirmed in the first sentence (see 1). 'All anecdotal interest is thus eliminated (Kristeva, 1980a: 42). Investors would certainly know that the measure would be defeated since Nike employees control 69 percent of the stock, of which half is owned by Phil Knight. The writer is left with an obvious conclusion, and the thematic axis is hardly news: the distance between executives and Asian worker compensation has a long history in reported Nike stories. This opposition telegraphs several related oppositions that appear in the 17 sentences (male/female, rich/poor, American/Asian, celebrity/other, old/young, etc.). Each sentence can be doubly interpreted with audience destinations to either term of the numerous dualities. The writer has no story, except that there is a carnivalistic play in the ambiguity of the oppositions that sets up the space for a middle ground or a resolution of the opposed terms, a repositioning of Nike's symbolic image to investors and consumers. The release ends abruptly on this note, with the visible absence of the swoosh logo and the 'Just Do It' slogan from the event.

We can also look at the history of pay raises for Asian workers. The release includes the speech that 'Nike will announce soon another pay raise for its Indonesian workers, after the 15 percent raise mandated by Indonesian authorities last spring, Eitel said.' There is always more to the story. The factory in Jakarta had to be shut down after more that 5,000 workers burned cars and ransacked offices to protest that Nike subcontractors were not paying them a $2.50 per day minimum wage. The factory had been refusing to pay a government-decreed minimum wage of $2.50 per day that took effect April 1:

> Jim Small said Saturday that the workers who struck the factory already were making more than the minimum wages and were upset because they expected a larger pay rise than there were given. He said the workers had expected a 10.6 percent pay raise but were given a 7.25 percent raise. He said all sides in the dispute planned to meet Monday. 'Nike officials are meeting with the factory management and are encouraging a solution to this,' Small said. 'It obviously is disturbing to us but at the same time it's part of collective bargaining.' He said the workers would be paid for the three days the factory is shut down.... On Tuesday, 13,000 workers from the same factory and other neighboring shoe and apparel plants held a six-mile-long protest march to demand higher wages. (CLR and Oregonian, 26 April 1997)

A pay raise may still mean that Nike is paying out less money, given the Indonesian inflation rate:

> The exchange rate in 1997 was 2,909 rupiah to the dollar, rising to 10,078 rupiah to the dollar in 1998. So the rupiah lost 70 percent of its value in dollar terms in one year. Nike claims it paid its Indonesian workers 137,500 rupiah per month in mid-1997. $137,500/2,909 = 47.27 per month; $47.27 \times 12 = $567.21/\text{year}$; $567.21/52 = $10.91/\text{week}$; $10.91/40 = 27$ cents an hour. (National Labor Committee, December 4, 1998. 'The NLC's response to Nike's Wage-Raise Press Release' *http://www.nlcnet.org/nike/wagememo.htm* Note the figures reported here come from the Economist Intelligence Unit, Ltd.)

Or we could look to Vietnam pay raises. 'Vietnam Labor Watch received a new stack of paystubs today from Vietnam. Nike workers there did get a 5% wage increase. They are now getting $47 per month, an increase of $2. Not all is good news, however.' Nike managers have their ways of countering a pay raise. 'Supposedly, salaries are deducted for mistakes made by workers. "Mistakes" however are defined by the companies i.e. "breaking needle," talking to other workers, leaving factory grounds for lunch' (CLR, 18 October 1997).

On March 19, 1999, Nike issued a press release indicating that Maria Eitel, Nike's vice president for corporate responsibility had given a speech to the Portland City Club outlining details of a wage increase for Indonesian workers. The release stated the raise was for 'entry-level cash wages for its Indonesian footwear factory workers from 250,000 Rupiah (Rp) to 265,000 Rp per month.... Before today's wage package, this segment of workers had received two wage increases (April/October, 1998) totaling 45%.' An activist group countered with its own press release: 'Nike Increases Wages by a Penny an Hour in Indonesia – Raising Wages from 14 cents to 15 cents an Hour – and issues a press release outlining Nike's "Social Responsibility Agenda."'

- A penny an hour increase: Nike workers in Indonesia now earn 15 cents an hour, and $6.07 a week.
- While announcing its 6 percent wage increase, Nike forgot to mention that the inflation rate in
- Indonesia was 54 percent in 1998, and that the local currency lost 70 percent of its value. In fact, in dollar terms, Nike has slashed wages 45 percent from 27 cents an hour in mid-1997 to the current 15 cents.
- In the last quarter, Nike's profits were up 70 percent, which – no doubt – helped pay the way for the 1 cent wage increase.
- The direct labor cost to assemble a $90 pair of Nike sneakers is approximately $1.20, which means that the workers' wages amount to just 1.3 percent of the retail price.

Summary

Intertextuality is a web of complex inter-relationships ensnaring each story's historicity and situational context between other stories. Essentially, every story is informed by other stories that the writer and reader have heard or read, and their respective cultural contexts. Intertextuality is an example of antenarrative analysis. Indeed every word in a story is contextualized by innumerable sources of experience, including any knowledge of shared or popular cultural references, what we know of characters, setting, prior events, storyteller, and what we anticipate will become text. Texts and narratives are not necessarily written, and as Kristeva indicates all signifying systems, from table settings, buildings, dances to poems, are constituted by the manner in which they transform earlier signifying systems.

If we look at the term 'intertextuality', it is a signifying system suspended in its own historicity. Kristeva substituted 'intertextual' for Bakhtin's (1986) word 'translinguistic' when reading a paper he wrote in the early 1950s. And I am writing this history of 'intertextuality' by summarizing other texts (i.e. Fairclough, 1992: 101–2; Stam et al., 1992: 206–10; Chandler, 1996). And my fragments of intertextual writings will become a link in a chain of someone else's writing on intertextuality.

The production of texts on intertextuality for Bakhtin, Kristeva, Fairclough and now me has both a 'horizontal' and a 'vertical' dimension. Horizontally a text is a link of a chain of texts that precede and proceed it in linear time. An obvious example is the references, footnotes, quotation marks and, more recently, hyper-links that incorporate one text into another. On the other hand, the vertical dimension of intertextuality refers to time-scales other than linear and to parameters that network a text to its contemporaries, as well as to other genres, discourses, styles and activities (Fairclough, 1992: 103). An example is the juxtaposition of one text with another such as in Derrida's writing or more recently with Burrell (1998). As I write this text on intertextuality, I am reaccentuating various quoted, summarized, (inadvertently) plagiarized and forgotten textual fragments into this heterogeneous accumulation. The methodological task is to unravel a text's intertextual network of attributed and unattributed links to other texts. Horizontally, we trace the transformations of an intertextual network over time, and vertically we trace its juxtaposition with other texts that constitute its changing identities.

In Chapter 6 I will look at causality, the narrative claims about event sequences and plots. Causality has a narrated quality, but it is also ante-narrative in the ways people posit causal assertions. Here too is an intertextual weave to be explored.

6

Causality analysis

Narrating fashions chains of causal assertions that can be analysed as an antenarrative system of claims and counter-claims. Nietzsche was among the first to question a universalized theory of causality:

> 'Causality' eludes us; to suppose a direct causal link between thoughts, as logic does – that is the consequence of the crudest and clumsiest observation. Between two thoughts all kinds of affects [sic] play their game: but their motions are too fast, therefore we fail to recognize them, we deny them. (Nietzsche, 1967: section 477)

Nietzsche (1956/1887: 209–10) muddies the causal waters and introduces an antenarrative position. He asked the question does cause lead to effect, or does effect lead to a search for cause? Or in chains of reinterpretation is cause–effect invented to impose our will to power? Here we are interested in how storytelling is laced with causal assertion: 'A' happened, 'B' must be the cause. We are also interested in how narrative causality analysis, for example, using a causal map methodology, erects an artificial narrative, an analyst narrative to replace acts of situated storytelling and antenarrating. In this sense we are interested in recovering antenarrative causality, the acts of storytelling that construct and reconstruct causality over time.

A narrative explains the 'why': what caused a series of events or phenomena to happen, unfold and end the way they did? Yet as Nietzsche reminds us (1967: 551) causality is an 'invention: a projection of our will onto an event, making some other event responsible for something that happens'. 'Causation involves a narrative structure in which we posit first the presence of a cause and then the production of an effect' (Culler, 1981: 183). Calling the causal narration of organizing into question is an antenarrative analysis.

When an *effect* is narrated as a consequence of a prior condition we invent stories of 'cause' that are at times fictive since they retrospectively narrate causality. The retrospective narrative that grasps a plot of cause and effect chaining and our questioning of that chaining as a fictive retrospective reconstruction is antenarrative. As Nietzsche put it: 'Interpretation by causality [is] as deception' (1967: 551).

Narration fears antenarrative moments where causal narration has not rendered experience into coherent patterns. Our fear of the chaotically unfamiliar, to explain world effects narratively by identifying their most probable cause or causes, masks the situated contexts of anti-narration. I have grown up to accept the semiotics of mechanistic interpretations of causality. My hard work in the office should cause me to get a raise, to live the fruits of the good life. 'A' caused 'B' and I am the human agent who did the work that led to the raise. But somehow the good life is always being shattered by contingency, and the causal field is messy and often unfathomable. Is it my belief in the force of my work, the equity of my organization or the skilled observation of my department head?

Empirically, causal analysis attempts to relate two events in a haphazard world by asserting the occurrence of one event to be the mechanical reason for the occurrence of the other. But in a world of multiplicities do we ever know what caused something to happen? The narrative acts of retrospective causality destroy the antenarrative experience of multi-causality and non-linear causality, and situations where the only cause is a fictive one. For example, did my dad's Corvair engine blow up because it leaked oil and I did not heed the flashing 'oil low' light on the dash, or was I getting even? Did the motor freeze because the car was not well maintained, or was it some spontaneous mechanical failure or driver-error? Or did I make up the story to cover up something else? There are times when I do not know exactly what caused some event. I may think two events or processes are connected, but the connection is a mystery or I prefer to story them mysteriously.

Physics is moving beyond mechanistic interpretation to more non-linear models, and organization studies follows along. We in organization studies are giving more sensitivity to initial conditions, self-organization and emergent dynamics in chaos and complexity theory. In the postmodern world of storytelling organizations linear causality is a convenient fiction, an over-simplified narrative of complex antenarrative dynamics in which non-linearity (and that too is a fiction) reigns. Organization studies are beginning to wrestle with an antenarrative understanding of causality. As Langley says, 'Researchers are also increasingly recognizing that the presence of multilayered and changing contexts, multidirectional causalities, and feedback loops often disturb steady progression toward equilibrium' (1999: 692).

We search for retrospective judgments about cause, effect, outcome and blame. We make attributions of cause and effect relations after the fact. In an antenarrative analysis of causality the focus is on when they were mere probabilities and guesses the time before they became stereotypes, ideologies and causal fixity.

We are taught to be aware of the difference between our causal mapping and unproven issues of causality. On a research methods listserv, (http://www.aom.pace.edu/rmd) I read the following:

> There are supposed to be several different studies, not all full two year longitudinal, that purport to show some negative social skills and social activities

correlations with internet use. Of course correlation alone usually leaves unproven the issues of causation. (3 February 2000)

A standard narrative analysis consists of identifying through content analysis the causal assertions in various texts and composing these into aggregate causal maps of the firm. An antenarrative approach views causal assertions as portals into an intertextual world (see Chapter 5), for example, linking the various types of assertion across intertexts (i.e. how one text interprets that causality in another text).

In Chapter 7 I note that people's ideas about time and the emplotment of an antecedent events to succeeding events can be analysed using ante-narrative assumptions of causality. Here I analyse how causal assertions are textual and intertextually constructed and reconstructed. This can mean some antecedent event was thought to explain the manifestation of an event in the present. And as time passes, the causal map gets reinterpreted and reinvented with new pathways. I do not want to forget to self-reflect on how I am constructing causal assertions in this text by producing narrative structures to persuade you that my antenarrative reading of various textual fragments of the causal retrospection processes can be privileged.

What is a causal assertion?

A simple definition is the principle that an antecedent event can be necessary and sufficient for the occurrence of a subsequent event, or that a set of events is thought to be chained together (e.g. as in a linear progression). Tobacco companies claim that no causal link has been proven between smoking and lung cancer.

Various ideologies of causality have become more or less fashionable in our science (Cook and Campbell, 1979). However, philosophical and methodological arguments over causality, its definition, or whether it even exists have raged for centuries. In organizational studies much of the debate is over mechanistic versus probability and co-occurrence (correlation) uses.

The usual disclaimer: 'co-occurrence is not proof of causality'

How many times do we hear this phrase in graduate school? We are taught in statistics courses if we observe that event 'C' always happens soon after event 'B', we cannot validly infer that event 'B' causes event 'C'. There may be some prior event 'A' that causes both 'B' and 'C', with no causal relation between 'B' and 'C'. For Max Weber, there is a probability of 'A' causing 'B'. In our method classes we are taught to write 'in so far as there is a probability that A caused B' rather than say 'A caused or determined B.' Weber believed in multi-causality and mutual causality systems (with lines in both directions), and in the probability of various interacting events, rather than the certainty of any one event. Marx on the other hand, viewed material conditions as a fundamental causal source (Coser, 1977). In their book *Connections: New Ways of Working in the*

Networked Organization, Sproull and Kiesler (1992) observe that Internet meetings are said to be positively associated with people being more open and free to give their real opinions. But, is this a causal or probability assertion? In social science we are careful to make such distinctions, but in everyday affairs, perhaps not as cautious.

What are types of causality?

In the acts of retrospective sensemaking we shall look at three types of causality:

1. Physical or generative causality
2. Psychological causality
3. Successionist causality (a mid-range theory between the first two)

Physical or generative causality
There are physical (generative) causes, such as the cue stick tapping the cue ball that hits the six ball that bounces off a rail and sinks the eight ball. Socrates (then Hobbes) described generative causality where every effect must have a cause. René Descartes also believed that a (mechanical) cause must contain the qualities of the effect or the power to produce the effect. This continued into the mechanistic age of science and Newtonian physics. Events must narrate mechanical causes.

Physical scientists of the seventeenth and eighteenth centuries took the mechanical view of causality as common sense. They reduced cause to a motion or change in motion resulting in other motions that could be described with mathematical precision. And John Stuart Mill sought to justify belief in universal (generative) causation on such empiricist principles. In sum the generative or mechanistic and determinist theory of causality is the cause of any event is a prior event without which the event in question could not have happened. This sets our opportunity for antenarrative analysis, the questioning of mechanistic causality.

Generative causality is a narrative in which cause generates its effects since cause and effect have a 'real' and 'mechanical' connection. Cause and effect are not independent events, or co-occurrent as Weber discussed (Coser, 1977). The narrative reconstructs the story of event 'A' and event 'B' with an attributed linkage mechanism. 'A' must cause 'B' because there is a mechanical link 'C'. Theories can also be generative narratives. For the Greek philosopher Aristotle, a general 'idea' and a particular 'phenomenon' had a connection that could be logically deduced (deductively reasoned).

Aristotle (in the classical *Politics*) enumerated four types of generative cause:

1. **Material cause** – What anything is made of – for example, brass or marble is the material cause of a given statue. Or the type of technology

determines the structure of the firm, or environment causes structure and process formation.

2. **Formal cause** – The agent who acts on the material, giving it form or pattern; thus, the designer of an organization would be its formal cause or, the CEO is the formal cause of strategic implementation.
3. **Efficient cause** – The immediate agent acting to produce the work or form, such as acts of supervision that motivate others' performance, or the manual energy of the labourers that cause quality in TQM.
4. **Final cause** – The end or motive for the sake of which the work is produced – that is, the pleasure of Bill Gates in seeing his vision of Microsoft realized.

Thus, in some organization theories, a firm is made up of communication networks among organs that are determined by environmental contingency, its material cause. The efficient cause is its founding narrative, who founded it: the formal cause is its species, or the industry or population it inhabits; and, its final cause is the motivational drive and need strengths that differentiate high and low performers.

There are other classifications of causality that can be assessed. One way to cluster causal assertions is into one of several types of cause:

1. **Necessary cause** – Must be present for the effect to occur, but by itself cannot produce the effect. Hierarchy, for example, is necessary to produce authoritarianism, but by itself cannot. Other factors are needed: a culture of superiors and subordinates, status inherent in offices, and people socialized to be authoritarian.
2. **Contributory cause** – May lead to an effect but cannot produce it by itself. For example, patriarchy may contribute to hierarchy, but subsystems and a division of labour are also important. Other disciplinary mechanisms (as listed by Foucault) must proliferate to sustain hierarchy.
3. **Sufficient cause** – Can produce an effect by itself. A micro-managing leader is sufficient to cause and produce hierarchy. All decisions must pass through a central point. Micro-managing is however not a 'necessary cause' of hierarchy, hierarchy may result from other causes such as the ideology of an institution such as in the example of the Catholic Church, with biblical interpretations and the pronouncements of the Vatican Council. A poorly implemented, micro-management bishops and popes might be a 'contributory cause' for continued hierarchy or help sustain its recreation.
4. **Remote cause** – One that is distant from an effect. A micro-manager in unit A is remote to the hierarchy forming in unit B. Hierarchy in China is a remote cause for hierarchy in Brazil. There may be imitation, as when a firm de-layers its hierarchy since it is fashionable in the industry to do so. But the mechanism linking the events has not been specified. In chaos theory, the butterfly can flap its wings, but the typhoon in Brazil must have some linking forces that come into play.

5. **Proximate cause** – Various events and states happen in near hierarchy: 'isolation, alienation, rigidity, resistance to change'. These are proximate causes, or close to the effect of hierarchy, but without being necessary, contributory or sufficient causes. You can have rigidity, resistance, etc. without having hierarchy, but hierarchy may exacerbate the effects.

Each of these types of cause is of concern to a theory of generative causality. For example, the Board of Trustees fired the president of the university because as some say he said in a press conference: 'If Ted Turner gives this university a donation the check will be deposited before the ink is dry.' His utterance shocked and offended the ranchers who control the board. We do not know without further inquiry if this was a necessary, contributory, sufficient, remote or proximate cause.

For it to be a necessary cause, we would need to know if the president's utterance was grounds for dismissal. I do know that one of the trustees published a newsletter to farmers and ranchers of New Mexico stating that when Ted Turner spoke on campus, the administration would not be accepting any checks. This may have prompted the reporter's question. It is likely, however, that there were other contributory causes to the firing. For example, our university only has five trustees, and the governor does the appointments, making it easy to get a majority decision. It is feasible that a micro-managing Board of Trustees was a sufficient cause. The event of the press conference and the firing were proximate, happening within a few days of each other.

Narrating particular events is subjective but can get presented in a text (like this example) as highly objective and factual. Any number of factors could have caused (contributed) to this outcome, but, over time one narrative account does tend to be repeated and widely accepted as fact. Details of collective memory, what was necessary, contributory, sufficient or proximate get forgotten.

From an antenarrative perspective we question accounts of generative causality by challenging them as fictive reification. There was no way to know what went on behind the closed doors of the Board of Trustees, so many experts narrated their accounts (including this one).

We remember Washington Irving's story of Christopher Columbus, and many forget to read the historical record of acts of kidnap, torture and murder on this 'great' voyage of (non-)discovery. This is the definition of reification, taking a subjective notion of the relation between events, forgetting the past and alternative accounts, and rendering stories as objective narration. Such reifications, conversions of stories to narrative, are ubiquitous in the everyday life of complex organizations. And they do mask the antenarrative mire.

Psychological causality
Beyond the mechanistic/physical causal schemes, there are 'psychological' causes, such as a personality that cannot resist the addiction to gambling.

Causal cognition is increasingly recognized as a central topic in psychology and in organization studies. People widely believe that in the course of natural events, there must be causal origins. In the case of the firing of the university president, some say there was a conflict of personalities among those newly appointed to the Board of Trustees. The climate changed and the press conference utterance was a triggering event (not sufficient in and of itself, but perhaps significant in contribution). For every human action there is by some accounts a determining psychological profile, a Myers-Briggs test to predict human sociability. Socially, a good deal of narrating is about profiling psychological essentialism, pigeon-holing people into boxes, assigning blame for some mistake or disaster, attributing cause to psychological maps. And in causal map analysis, the psychological profile is captured in architectural display. An antenarrative analysis would focus instead on how we arrived at our causal mapping and its narration. Retrospective causal explanations of essentialist psychological profile are considered here to be reified acts of narration, substitutes to erase and forget multiple and more subjective stories.

Successionist causality
The successionist theory, exemplified by David Hume (1711–76), posited that causality was not a real phenomenon, but somewhere between the fiction of mind and the coincidence of occurrences. As such, this approach to causality is a mid-range theory between generative and pure psychological causality. Henri Bergson (1910) also contended that ultimate reality or life is not bound by exact causal sequences. Rather, antecedent events and conditions need not produce the exact same results. This approach anticipates current complexity theory notions of causality as emergent patterns that can vary from common initial conditions or starting points.

Successionist causality in narrative terms is an account more similar to Weber's correlation. A cause is narrated as something that was a statistically probable event, happening just before some effect. Cause and effect events are therefore assumed to be independent or their specific connection unknowable (at least by the method in use). People make causal attributions of a link between 'A' and 'B' when there may not be anything more than coincidence or prejudice manifest. Since the ground is changing, narrations of causal attributions are acts of misplaced concreteness.

For Nietzsche (1956/1887), causality was not always a case of cause leads to effect. In his famous example of the mosquito, we are bitten (effect happens) and we look about for a cause (there is a mosquito). We then make the attribution of causality. Nietzsche did not buy into a linear theory of causality. Instead he advocated a circular theory of events in which eternal recurrence was a central concept.

Chaos and causality
Several postmodern insights appear to have unseated both principles of causality from their previously unquestioned position. In chaos and

complexity theory, a given cause may have any one of a number of effects, which one of those effects will occur cannot be predicted, even in principle. In addition there is an assumption of non-linearity. And a butterfly flapping its wings in China can cause a chain of events that lead to a hurricane in Florida. The word 'causal' may be appropriate in physics, where stress causes instantaneous strain and vice versa, but one should return to the less mechanistic words in social science. But even in post-Newtonian physics, causality has been redefined since Einstein's relativity theory into the new complexity theories.

Approaches to narrative causality

The next sections look at two approaches to narrative causality: stream analysis and causal map aggregation. In both cases, we will examine ante-narrative alternative analyses.

Stream analysis and causality

Jerry Porras developed an approach to causality that crosses causality and story analysis in his book *Stream Analysis: A Powerful Way to Diagnose and Manage Organizational Change* (1987). Stream analysis begins with the assumption that problems, events, people and routines in organizations are interconnected and networked. The ultimate goal of stream analysis is to systematically chart chains of cause and effect that cross boundaries of function and structure. The end result is a series of narratives about stream maps. The end result is to generate a chart of ideal streams (or physical and psychological links in our terms) so that change strategies can be invented to move and change beyond the current stream. Material and formal causal maps (in our language) are erected to allow efficient and final changes.

The analysis proceeds by setting out problems prominent in an organization and sorting them into causal categories such as technical, physical setting, administrative, social system, etc. Then lines of causal probability are drawn to map a problem stream where causality needs to get pinned down. Finally, there is story charting, where traces of the interconnection of a given problem to other problems (events, people and routines) are depicted. In our language, this is a narrative, an account that stands in substitution for stories of the situation. The approach has been said to be quite popular with engineers. A skeptical reading is that the world of systems engineering is juxtaposed in stream analysis with a deterministic and even material theory of narrative causality. However, an alternate reading is that stream analysis is the tracing of interconnections among events thought to be discrete and isolated. The analyst (with joint involvement of system engineers) traces how events from one domain (unit, team, department, level, contract or layer) are narrated as interconnected to some other domain. An event of the one type (e.g. technology that breaks down) has occurred when the circumstances are logically independent of narratives such that a distinct event of the other type (e.g. training of operators) has occurred in the circumstances. And there could be alternative narratives composed to explain the breakdown, lack of maintenance, faulty parts, over-use, etc. at issue for us. To what extent are the stream charts displacements of a more ethnographic look at the embedded storytelling streams? An alternative analysis would trace the ongoing constructing and reconstructing of narrative maps of the system by participants as well as by stream analysts.

Causal maps

Axelrod's (1976) analysis of 'causal maps' looks at how people cognitively form relations between concepts and events. Nodes are used to represent concepts and signed arcs to depict either positive or negative causal relations. Individual maps can then be analysed for similarities and differences. Interview transcripts can code concepts and posited relationships to construct cognitive maps. These maps are assumed to depict the reality constructions of the organization members. 'Cause maps' (or attention maps in Huff's (1990) terms) capture a person's worldview as a cognitive structure consisting of causally interconnected sets of concepts (Lee et al., 1992). Cause maps of interviews were 'funneled' together to erect aggregate causal maps of the entire organization in a recent study (Klimecki and Lassleben, 1998). Their qualitative analysis constructs a narrative of the organizations learning system:

> We described the cognitive contents by funneling interview data into cognitive maps, and the communication relations by casting them into networks. On this basis, further descriptive measures, referring to contents as well as to structures, and facilitating the analysis and comparison of the two OL systems, were derived.
>
> Regarding the contents of the organizational maps, we identified the dominating concepts. As to the organizational maps of attention, this was done by ranking concepts according to degree of sharedness and total frequency. For the organizational cause maps the same procedure was applied, separately for cause concepts, effect concepts and causal relations, thus detecting main causes, main effects and main relations. (Klimecki and Lassleben, 1998: 419–20)

The content of the narrative is 'composed of (row sums), and central addresses, shown by indegrees (column sums), within each network' (Klimecki and Lassleben, 1998: 415–20). The analysts argue that organizational learning is the transformation of causal maps of reality that is shared among organizational members. This inductive, theory building research is described as qualitative, but its actions are decidedly quantitative. Next, we examine what an antenarrative causal analysis would entail.

Antenarrative causality

In narrative texts, there are frequent utterances of a causal nature. But, do we aggregate them into causal maps or streams charts and posit a universal narrative of the entire firm? Narrative is a plausible and sometimes fantastic explanation of personal or social motivations and factors that create emotions, moods or actions. But funneled into analyst aggregations what have we got? A universalized account of how 'A' caused 'B', and 'A' can be a person, market, institution, atmosphere, etc. Event 'B' can be some kind of change of state in these same phenomena. The picture is too tidy; it sweeps aside the random occurrence, coincidence, mis-attributions, and we are left with over-determined constructions rendered by the analysts' and their software. An antenarrative analysis would call into question mechanical as well as successionist accounts of causality. It would also question how causal assertions are made and what they mean when analytically aggregated into causal maps or stream charts to render the entire organization, as illustrated in the previous examples. We are therefore concerned with narrated attributions of causality, not with proving their reality but in recovering their storied circumstances. The analysis proceeds in several antenarrative processes that attempt to trace causal assertions in narratives:

1. Identifying temporal language in narratives
2. The relation between microstories and macrostories
3. Tracing intertextual linkages of assertions across stories
4. Developing a narrative mapping of causal assertions

Identifying temporal language in narratives
In a narrative text, there are accounts of assertions of 'possible' transitions and relations between events in the world that have historical origins. One place to begin is to look for uses of temporal language. Our personal ideology of time and causality can get us into trouble. We may believe an event is said to immediately precede another and to anticipate some future event. The narrative can impose order when there is none, and at some point the narrators may proscribe that state changes are somehow deterministic.

In the linear Aristotelian narrative form we are quite familiar with in Hollywood movies, events at the beginning cause those in the middle, and events in the middle cause those at the end (Chandler, 1996). We may seek out only those utterances that construct an intrinsic temporal direction into the structure of the narrative. The problem we face is that various authors have their own ideology of time and may not be using this familiar narrative structure. Nietzsche (1956/1887) reminds us that one perceived ordering of cause leading to effect can have no more reality than its converse: we experience an effect and seek its cause. In the laws of mechanical physics we may conceive of time as 'moving linearly forward' but time is a human construct. The new physics conceives of time as non-linear. Many cultures ascribe a cyclical time. A narrative may story causality as operating in a circular-time in which our future provides the cause of the world states in our past. My point is we need to look at the specific type of time theory (linear, non-linear, circular, etc.) that is being narrated. The narrative concept of time may be quite unfaithful to temporal reality. Temporality is an internal relation and construction of the textuality of the narrative. We analyse each narrative to see if the time between two world states is narrated as causally connected? What is the 'flow' of time narrated in the text?

We will take the Nike and activists texts as our example so we can outline each step of causal assertion and time analysis (Boje, 1998b, c, d, e, f, g, 1990, 2000c, d, e). For example, the activist narrative takes a generative view of causality that holds that the nature of Nike as an organization determines what specifically will happen in a given set of circumstances in Asian factories (Harré, 1985). For example, if we look at several Nike texts, they posit causal assertions as to why their overseas operations are not sweatshops. Alternatively, various protest groups and media texts posit just these same factories are sweatshops. Each of the texts (Nike and others) presents various textual evidence to back up and defend its causal assertions. One analysis would be to focus on the types of causal assertion being made and classify them into a taxonomy of thematic structures. What are the necessary and contributory, remote and proximate causal assertions? What may initially appear to be very different narratives of sweatshop attribution may utilize similar narrative structures (i.e. the linearity of time and the causal clusters).

Nike, on the other hand, narrates a successionist view of causality asserting that there is no relationship between the Nike Corporation and the statistical occurrences of negative labour practices (denying as well any necessary, sufficient cause or even contributory cause). The generative and successionist assertions of causality made by activists resist vehemently Nike's theory of causality. For the activists, Nike's existence is contributory to sweatshop formation among sub-contract factories because of Nike's anti-labour organizing actions and wage policies. Nike on the other hand claims it is a remote player, and that if anything negative is occurring in the factories the sub-contractors are proximate to the events in question.

Activists counter that since Nike policies give sub-contractors little or no option to construct factory situations that do not generate poor labour practices, Nike is not as remote as Nike press releases contend. Nike, by contrast, attributes poor conditions to proximate effects, the host country's failed economy, government corruption and traditions of authoritarian control.

From Nike press releases, the cause and effect linkages exist only in the minds of the activists, certain media writers and overactive imaginations of university students and their professors. To Nike, there are no logical causal connections between Nike policies and actions and Asian factory conditions. Nike further contends there is no uniform culture of expectations and norms across the globe, and that it is therefore inappropriate to hold up Western culture as the measure for Asian culture.

The relation between macro and micro-storytelling
Within a text we seek causal relations between macro and micro-accounts. There are intertextual chains of assertions in narratives such as 'A' provides causal support to 'B' and 'B' to 'C'. For example, most organization theories explicitly or implicitly equate 'hierarchy' with authoritarianism, domination, patriarchy and rigidity. Two or more causal effects can be chained in a narrative of causality, for example, hierarchy causes domination, patriarchy and rigidity. 'A' provides causal support for both 'B1', 'B2' and 'B3'. Alternatively, 'B1', 'B2' and 'B3' provide causal support for 'A': in short, there are mutual causal assertion theories of hierarchy.

Example: micro and macro-storytelling and causal assertion Activists and Nike frame the microstories into more macro-interpretations of Nike's role in the global economy (Boje, 1999c). Nike tells romantic tales of utopian and economic progress. Activists, by contrast, tell stories of Nike's anti-democratic and colonialist anti-development of Third World economies. The postmodern storytelling being lived out by entrepreneurial activists and Nike as they each seek to expose the biased, dualistic, deterministic, uni-causal–effect scenarios and plot structures of the other. In this tactic, they reframe the microstories as a macrostory of very different meaning. For example, in the 'Nike Index' story, Nike is the change agent of economic development in the Third World:

> In simplest terms, the Nike Index tracks a developing economy's economic development by Nike's activity in each country. Economic development starts when Nike products are starting to be manufactured there (Indonesia, 1989; Vietnam, 1996). The economy hits the second stage – development at a level where per capita income indicates labor flowing from basic industries like footwear and textiles to advanced industries like electronics and cars (Hong Kong, 1985; Korea, 1990); and an economy is fully developed when Nike had developed that country as a major market (Singapore, 1991; Japan, 1984; Korea, 1994). (Nike Web, 1998, http://cbae.nmsu.edu/~dboje/NIKfaq.html)

Philip Knight at the September 1997 stockholders' meeting restoried microstories of corporal punishment into a second macrostory of how developing countries are 'growing up' with Nike's leadership:

> The process of having managers from foreign countries overseeing those 500,000 workers is somewhat difficult for all of us, but over the next two or three years, you will see that process change as the knowledge of the workers gets better, the management talents grow up, and they come to be managed by countries of their own nation – by citizens of their own nation. (see appendix of Landrum, Nancy (2000) dissertation study)

Activists also tell macrostories, for example, an anti-democracy spin is laid on the Nike Index (macrostory) of economic development:

> The Jardine and Fleming [one of Hong Kong's largest investment houses] report is titled 'Tracking Nike's Footprints Across Asia.' The Jardine and Fleming report emphasizes: 'If we delve deeper into where Nike has produced sneakers and its comments about political stability, we notice that Nike tends to favor strong governments. For example, Nike was a major producer in both Korea and Taiwan when these countries were largely under military rule. It currently favors China, where the Communists and only two men have led the country since 1949, and Indonesia where President Suharto has been in charge since 1967.... Likewise, Nike never did move to the Philippines in a big way in the 1980s, a period when democracy there flourished. Thailand's democracy movement of 1992 also corresponded to Nike's downgrading of production in that country.' When democracy rears its head, Nike takes a hike. (Silverstein and Cockburn, 1997)

Again, entrepreneurial-activist, Thuyen Nguyen (24 July 1997g), gets into the act by pointing out how (micro) stories of worker abuse are rationalized away by Nike's officials' bottom line (macro) stories of industry structure, manufacturing chains, developing country woes, and the bottom line.

> The main reason can be found in the industry's business structure. The current relationship between buyers, contractors, subcontractors and inspectors often ignores the interest of workers. This might be the most profitable way to organize the industry but this structure gives no voice to workers. At each link on the manufacturing chain, there is always some other factors that are more important than the worker's interests i.e. profit, production, quality, shipping deadline or monthly quota. It becomes too easy for a company on this chain to pay attention to the bottom line rather than to worry about some poor women. Especially in an under-developed country, it is always easy to rationalize away the fact that she might be slapped occasionally, but without a job she would be hungry.

These macrostories and counter-stories set off chaos patterns. The local stories of worker abuse crafted by entrepreneurial activists, such as Ms Benjamin Medea and Thuyen Nguyen, are embedded in a macrostory about the workings of Nike's global enterprise and economic development (this is a renarrating of a Nike story by Silverstein and Cockburn, 1997):

> Nike factory, Knight argues, should be viewed as a kind of internship, the skimpy paycheck a passport for a better future. 'We give people a chance to work themselves out of poverty,' Knight professed. 'When their bellies are full and they've got a roof over their heads, only then can they think about changing their government.' (As a lesson in the new global economy, Knight's company charges its workers for drinking water.) 'Nike is US foreign policy in action,' Knight wrote in Nike's 1996 annual report.

By ignoring Aristotle's application of the Generative Law of Causality (defined above as a narrative in which cause generates its mechanistic effects) to corporate actions, Nike's causality is divorced from any direct connection to material conditions of labour and ecology in Asian sub-contract factories. If this view of causality is accepted, one cannot prove or validate the law of causality in accounts of successive events, such as by activists and media. Activists, on the other hand, appear to adopt a succession of events theory of causality in which labour practice events in Asia can be linked to Nike's antecedent policies and actions. The activists by noticing some regularity of Nike labour practices do not yet by those narratives yield an understanding of the material causative relationship of Nike and labour practices.

Tracing intertextual linkages of assertions across stories
As reviewed in Chapter 5, analysis can occur within a complex textual system and across the intertextual pathways between texts (see the AP and Nike press releases, above).

Hardly a day passes in which one does not read another example of Nike narrative that denies responsibility for overseas labour practices. And each line of a Nike press release can be read as a dialogic response to another text, in order to resituate assertions of agency, blame and causality. One text may argue the consequences of sweatshops are just the reverse of what is asserted by another text. Whether it is holding the sub-contractors and not Nike responsible for negative practices, blaming the media or activists for getting their facts wrong, or absolving itself of their acts because of other causal influences such as globalization, customs in a given country, or the vindictiveness of critics the idea that Nike is a primary cause is rejected. Nike's narrations and activists' counter-narratives have led to calls for independent monitoring by Nike stockholders and others. Nike counters by pointing out that they work directly with the US government and conform to wage and other labour practices of host countries, and further adds that it has been an industry leader in crafting codes of conduct and implementing progressive practices. How did this view of causality – one that ignores the role of Nike – gain such prominence? Activists, on the other hand, narrate a radically different theory of causality – one that places corporate and personal causal efficacy at Nike's feet. Nike succeeds in narrating itself into the opposite of what activists contend.

Developing a narrative mapping of causal assertions
A narrative mapping can display the linkages of the various causal assertions. Many believe that there are individual differences in people's causal understanding of how and why events occur (such as internal and external locus of control). A more impersonal orientation 'involves people's experiencing their behavior as being beyond their intentional control' (Deci and Ryan, 1985b: 112). What some see as an environmental threat, others see as a weakness to be controlled or an opportunity to be exploited. People high on internal control are more likely than others to exhibit the 'type A' behaviour pattern – a focus on pressure, tension and aggressive achievement (Deci and Ryan, 1985a).

However, for this analysis, I propose a narrative approach rather than a causal orientation survey or content analysis of assertion to fashion streams or causal maps. The challenge is to trace the situated assertions as they traverse and construct relationships in an interpersonal network. For example, do employees believe management's account of why the firm will be downsized and people laid off? Do employees attribute procedural fairness to the process? The analysis would mean collecting stories and reactions over time. Since organizational storytelling processes involve many voices, and non-linear relationships with fragmented feedback, tracing causal assertions may show a more varied pattern than the cognitive map approaches.

A variety of storied constructions may occur simultaneously among various portions of the organization with no shared map to be found. Storytelling is a way to make a meaningful connection between intra-organization, interorganizational and other environmental events. Langley (1999: 695–9) recommends a narrative strategy that would construct a detailed story from the raw data of history, in the style of Chandler's (1964) study of the evolution of American enterprise, and the invention of the 'M' form. Qualitative researchers argue that a 'contextualist' approach, one that generates richly textured understandings of context, is essential in this type of research (Pettigrew, 1985, 1990; Pettigrew and Whipp, 1991). An antenarrative analysis can do more than describe the event; it can, as Langley (1999) argues, dig below the surface of narrative to ascertain and ascribe causal patterns.

In sum, an antenarrative analysis looks at how people put fragments of story together into causal assertion. In what ways are naïve theories of causality posited in narratives? Are there generative and successionist utterances; can the assertions be contextualized? In what ways are statements necessary and sufficient or remote causal narrations? And how do narrative analysts fashion causal maps and statements about the firm as a whole? There seems to be a need to distinguish between narrative aggregation approaches aimed at quantification and those that can trace the antenarrative dynamics in play. The causal field is messy and often unfathomable and acts of narration camouflage that antenarrative fabric of complex organizations. In Chapter 7, I will embed causality in Ricoeur's theory of narrative emplotment. In Ricoeur's theory is an antenarrative position, one that views causality as an act of prenarrative knowledge, before plot is agreed.

7

Plot analysis

Relevant to organization studies is the question of who gets to author the narrative plot of complex organizations. A starting definition of plot that connects with Chapter 6 is the chaining of cause and effect or stimulus and response into a pattern, structure or network. Plot also relates to tracing the microhistory and textuality of relationships between obstacles to human intentions, antecedents, behaviour, contexts and outcomes in webs of other events.

A more comprehensive definition of plot is not just a chronology of events; it is what links events together into a narrative structure. And in antenarrative there is non-plot and contention over who controls plot as well as the embedded situation of how plots get worked out in social systems. To go beyond these initial definitions of plot we have to move from plot to Paul Ricoeur's 'emplotment'. Ricoeur also connects to themes from previous chapters: while he does not use the term 'intertextuality' he does employ the symbolic mediations of textual interweave, and the dialectic of text to world (mediated in other texts) and the relation between text and reader. Ricoeur also moves beyond a single story of history as we reviewed in grand narrative and does not abandon historiography or what we covered in microstoria (see Chapters 2 and 3). His theory of emplotment has a more comprehensive construct of time and narrative cause than we saw in Chapter 6 on causality.

Plots

We begin with an introductory taxonomy of ways narrativists 'emplot' stories into narratives based on Aristotle's classic typology of plots as comedic, tragic, romantic and ironic (or satiric) and adapted from Frye (1957), White (1978), and Frank (1995). My reading of Ricoeur's emplotment analysis follows this, with applications to organizations:

- **Romance** – Romance is a drama of self-identification symbolized by a heroine's victory over the world of experience. The hero is redeemed and/or liberated. Romance is the hero's transcendence through some progress quest to bring back what Joseph Campbell calls 'boon'.
- **Satire (irony)** – Satire/irony is the opposite of romance. It is a drama of apprehension symbolized by the heroine's captivity in the world.

S/he is never able to overcome the darkness, get out of the abyss. Satire exposes the 'ultimate inadequacy of the visions of the world' that posits harmony (White, 1973: 10). Postmodern ironic testimony is witness 'to a truth that is generally unrecognized or suppressed' (Frank, 1995: 137). That is, harmony is fictive illusion.

- **Comedy** – In comedy, there is hope for the heroes in a temporary triumph over darkness. Comedy offers temporary reconciliation or harmony. Reconciliations are symbolized by a festive occasion and harmony can be achieved between conflicting parties.
- **Tragedy** – In tragedy, the hero is defeated by the experiences of the world, yet hope exists for those left behind by their understanding of the limits of overcoming the abyss. Liberation is possible.

This ancient typology is relevant for contemporary organizational analysis, but I think it is made even richer by looking at Ricoeur's additions to plot. As a class assignment, we asked MBA students to read the above definitions and write about the plots in Karl Marx (1867). Several examples point out differences in how plot was seen in Marx's writing:

- **MBA 1** – Marx's plot of Chapter 10, 'The Working Day' is one of satire/irony as well as romance. Capitalism, as the hero, is trapped by greed into thinking of labour power as non-human, mechanistic. This is accomplished by repeatedly referring to capitalism as the 'were-wolf' as in '… [in] its were-wolf hunger for surplus-labour, capital oversteps not only the moral, but even the merely physical bounds of the working day.' – more evidence that capitalism has overlooked the 'festivals of local production and consumption' in exchange for the 'corporate imperialism spectacles of production and consumption'.
- **MBA 2** – From a sociological point of view, it would seem that Karl Marx is Plot in 'The Working Day' article as a tragedy. This is evidenced by his use of a tragic perspective of the working class to make his point known to the reader. Examples of such a tragic style are shown in his comments about the working class (labourers) being locked into a system of constant oppression by the wealthy. Marx further deduces that the power elite forces the labourers to work longer hours for the same pay claiming that there is a seemingly endless supply of labour which can be exploited by the powerful few. This is particularly evident in an ever-expanding imperialistic market where the affluent business owners become more wealthy while the labourers continue to languish in the bowels of poverty. Sentiments such as these are common throughout Marx's work as he advocates for a socialist based economy where power is distributed equally among the workers. Thus, Marx is also writing in a style which hints at the continual of hope found within the labour force, letting us know that we will be able to overthrow the constraints of the power elite and emerge as a new egalitarian commonwealth where every individual holds an equal stake in the wealth of

the society as a whole. With this is mind, he hopes for change, and feels that change is possible only if the right conditions are in place before this type of system can be implemented.

- **MBA 3** – I see Marx using a tragic plot in his description of the labourers in the nineteenth century. The labourers (whether they are men, women or children) are the heroes in Marx's story. The labourers have great odds to overcome as they are pitted against the greedy capitalists who are forever trying to get as much surplus working time out of the labourers, no matter what the cost to the labourers. Whose rights take precedence? Those of the labourers who want to be paid for the value of their labour, or those of the capitalists who purchase the labour and therefore believe they own it and can exploit it by extending the working day? What recourse of action do the labourers have? The capitalists do not honour the Factory Acts, nor do they show concern for the physical or mental health of the labourers. Instead, to the capitalists, these labourers are expendable. They are treated worse than slaves. The tragedy of the labourers is demonstrated by Marx's description of the good life of the blacksmith before capitalism, when he worked in moderation and had time for enough food and sleep. After he starts working for the capitalist, however, he dies young. Then there are the children who do not have the time for schooling. If the factory children know no other life besides work and are not educated, how will they ever be able to fight for their right to a better life?

- **MBA 4** – Marx's article would come under satire or irony, according to my understanding. Marx's plot of the nineteenth-century working life as a total misery. According to him the working class has been living like worse than animals. I agree with him in this regard but only to some extent. He portrays the workers as the slaves of the capitalists. It's true that the owners or the so-called vampires always think for their benefits and ignore the needs and wants of the labour class, but here the question is that, is this all due to the acts of the owners? I'm afraid not. I believe that the workers are also part of this discrimination. They let them rule and keep on working as slaves even after the Industrial Revolution. Inspite of all that, all my sympathies are still with the working class. The capitalists have been exploiting the workers for many centuries. While reading Karl Marx's article I found a bunch of quotes that represents capitalists as devils.... I totally agree with Marx while talking about the nineteenth-century working class, but we should come up with some solutions rather than criticizing the system. I think the working class should sit together and make their minds not to sell them and their families in the hands of the capitalists. I think that time is not very far when there will be great revolution by the workers and the capitalists will have to surrender.

- **MBA 5** – I found the reading from Marx this week to be most enjoyable. I found evidence of both irony and tragedy to be the most prevalent elements of plot. In several passages, Marx points out the irony of the capitalists milking the working class to exhaustion for all the surplus labour they can get: 'The same blind eagerness for plunder that in one case exhausted the soil, had, in the other, torn up by the roots the living force of the nation' and 'If then the unnatural extension of the working day, that capital necessarily strives after in it's unmeasured passion for self-expansion, shortens the length of life of the individual laborer, and therefore the duration of his labor power, the forces used up have to be replaced at a more rapid rate and the sum of the expenses for the labor power will be greater.' Nowhere in the chapter is irony more apparent then at the end when Marx points out 'that the time for which he (worker) is free to sell his labor-power is the time for which he is forced to sell it.' It is clear to me that much of the legislation passed to protect the working class from exploitation by the capitalists, ironically, did little to promote the freedom of the laborers, but rather served to strengthen limitation on that freedom for the good of the capitalists.

Marx's chapter on the working day laid out a perfect tragedy in addition to all the irony. The hero (the working class) is continually defeated by the capitalist machine from the fourteenth century through the nineteenth century. Yet, hope remains for modern culture to learn from the struggles of the heroes that have come before us and overcome the exploitations of the masses by the few.

- **MBA 6** – After reading some of the responses I would have to disagree about Marx. When I read the chapter it didn't seem to be a tragedy. I saw the workers liberation hard to obtain. I felt somewhat hopeless. I know he depicts some of the 'workers' victories' but the plot is so dark and depressing that liberation is something the workers have to struggle for indefinitely. He accomplished to plot the workers oppressed situation when he depicts greedy capitalists as vampires that would suck every drop of blood out of the workers. It seem to be more of a satire, where the heroes (workers) seem 'not to be able to overcome the darkness and get out of the abyss'. I guess we should read the whole book (*Capital*) to be able to see if Marx's theory offers an attainable solution. Then we could see his entire system as a whole and then see if we can categorize it as a tragedy.

Of course, we know he offers a 'solution' after reading *Capital*. His solution is Marxism. However, there seems to be something tricky about it. He began a revolution but I'm not sure he finished it. For me *Capital* is only the beginning of explaining the process of the workers' struggle. Workers have changed and will continue changing over time, they have different needs, different ways. Did Marx really provide room for those changes in his worker struggle system? Was his whole plot open for new kinds of struggle? Or did he get so caught up with the workers' situation at that time that he didn't foresee future changes? If I were to plot it again, I would provide for these changes. Marxism needs a resituation, one that leaves room for evolution looking at the struggle system as part of a whole organic system and not in a vacuum tube.

After the email-list postings and counter-postings of some thirty students, we had a lively class discussion about aspects of Marx we read as tragic, ironic/satiric or romantic. The class exercise, to me, is more than pedagogy. It illustrates that people disagree over plot. Next I will look at Ricoeur's theory of emplotment and what it adds to a typology such as Frye's.

From plot to emplotment

This conceptual bridge has three layers or 'unfolding representative stages' Ricoeur (1984) terms mimesis$_1$, mimesis$_2$, and mimesis$_3$. He offers a most rigorous discussion of plot in an effort to form a three-way conversation between phenomenology, narrative (literary criticism) and history. To do so he brings in Heidegger's *Being and Time* (1962) to build his mimetic, triadic bridge (and spiral) model of the structural relations between narrative and time. For Ricoeur 'emplotment' encompasses plot as an aspect of the second of three stages, a mediating moment in a hermeneutic 'bridge' of different mimetic circuits. The three mimetic stages for Ricoeur form a bridge between Augustine (three-fold present of time) and Aristotle (model of tragic, comedic, romantic and ironic plots). And it is in the second mimesis of emplotment (the grasping together of characters, plot, scenes, etc.) that plays its mediating role between time and narrative. First a brief overview followed by a more detailed explanation of the three stages.

In the first mimetic, we look to the pre-understanding of networks of action, symbolism and narrative time that are required to be able to emplot. This is the stage of prenarration, what we need to know to affix a plot. Secondly is the mimesis of emplotment, the grasping together of selected events, characters and actions into a plot line. Ricoeur relies on hermeneutics and Heidegger to pull together his approach to plot analysis. Thirdly is the final stage of mimesis that reconnects the parts to the whole into the hermeneutic circle.

Each mimesis has several sub-actors and structural hierarchies that are inter-related between the three moments. This triadic bridge of mimeses can be summarized: The dialectic of time and narrative depends on M_1, a preunderstanding (comprised of action network, symbolic mediation and narrative temporality), with M_2, emplotment (constituted by mediation of event and story, heterogeneous factors and synthesis of heterogeneity) together with M_3, temporality (of the hermeneutic circle in relation to the spiral of these three moments of mimesis).

And the model as a whole with parts is a spiral or hermeneutic circle. And it is a hermeneutic spiral of three stages that moves beyond the phenomenology of time, emplotment and the configuration of narrative in ways that allow us to theorize antenarrative. That is, the moments when there is not a sufficient pre-understanding to grasp together elements into a narrative emplotment. To understand this, what follows is a more complete examination of each stage.

Mimesis₁

For Ricoeur 'To imitate or represent action is to preunderstand what human acting is, in its semantics, its symbolic system, its temporality' (1984: 64). Plot in this first mimesis is defined as the ordering of action events, symbolism and temporality. And there are prenarrative experiences that refuse to be narrated (antenarrative). For example, Holocaust witnesses present us with chaotic gap, or a 'hole in the narrative that cannot be filled in' (Frank, 1995: 98). Those living in chaos only through retrospective and reflective glance turn chaos into narrative, but once mediated by narrative, it is no longer chaos. This prompts Frank to refer to the 'chaos narrative' as an *'antenarrative … a telling without mediation, and speaking about oneself without being fully able to reflect on oneself'* (1995: 98). Chaos is a prenarrated experience that is lived, but not told except in the 'syntactic structure of "and then and then and the"' (1995: 99). This unplotted storytelling presents us with a 'hole in the telling' (1995: 102). For Ricoeur (1984: 54–64) plots are constructed from pre-understandings of the following:

1. **Networks of action** – A network of actions implies goals, refers to motives and has agents responsible for various consequences. Preunderstanding networks question 'what', 'why', 'who', 'how', 'with whom', or 'against whom' in regard to a given action (Ricoeur, 1984: 55). In antenarrative these questions go answered. Practical understanding of action networks is necessary to achieve narrative understanding. A practical understanding of networks of action allows us to link questions of agent, goal, means, circumstance, help, hostility, cooperation, conflict, success, failure, etc. into a narrative understanding.
2. **Symbolic mediations** – Plots require a practical understanding and knowledge of the symbolic resources and processes of culture, the signs, rules and norms of a given context. Symbolic mediation is a focus on the symbols of a culture that underlie networks of action as meaningful articulations (1984: 57). For example, within cultures we value action networks and symbolize the ethical qualities of some actions as noble and others as vile, tragic or comedic. Action for Ricoeur 'can never be ethically neutral' (1984: 59).
3. **Temporal narration** – Plot requires a pre-understanding of time and temporal structures. This part of the bridge is constructed between 'Care' and the 'narrative order' of plot. Plot confers a sequential interconnection and integration on agents, deeds and their sufferings into temporal wholes, but does so with a sense of 'Care' (Ricoeur, 1984: 56–7, 64). Temporal structure networks of action and symbolic systems call for narrative Care. For Augustine narrative time was a 'threefold present, a present of future things, a present of past things,

and a present of present things' (Ricoeur, 1984: 60). In our 'vulgar' conception of linear time metrics we experience a simple succession of abstract 'nows' without a sense of 'Care' (Ricoeur, 1984: 62). Heidegger's concept of Care is essential to the definition of within-time-ness or being-within-time and is not to be confused with measuring time intervals. There is, for example, a temporal grammatical network of adverbs: 'then, after, later, earlier, since, until, so long as, during, all the while that, now that, etc' (1984: 62). There is a preoccupation with the character of being-within-time that is not to be confused with the things we Care about. Our preoccupations with being-within-time or the 'existential now' are for Ricoeur 'borrowed from the natural environment and first of all from the play of light and of the seasons' (1984: 63). Care is making-present, the three-fold presence of time. Being-within-time is not the same as Heidegger's concept of historicality.

Mimesis$_2$

Ricoeur prefers the word 'emplotment' to 'plot' for this stage of mimesis. Emplotment here is the 'grasping together' of the elements (events, factors and time episodes) to enact narrative configuration and thereby accomplish the mediation between the earlier and latter stages of mimesis. Emplotment is constructed out of M_1 this pre-understanding of networks of actions, symbolic mediation and being-within-time and a postunderstanding (M_3). There are three mediations to accomplish emplotment:

1. **Mediation between individual events and story as a whole** – A diversity of events or succession of incidents are constructed and grasped together into a meaningful story. An event has meaning in its relation to other events and incidents in the development of a plot within the meaningfulness of the whole story. Stories are more than a chronology of events in serial order because of plot, which organizes and (re)configures event networks into an intelligible whole.
2. **Mediation between heterogeneous factors** – Factors as heterogeneous as 'agents, goals, means, interactions, circumstances, unexpected results' get emploted and embellished. Plot (re)configures heterogeneous events and factors into a whole story and into one grand 'thought', 'point', or 'theme'.
3. **Mediation allows a synthesis of the heterogeneous** – The episodic dimensions of narrative are chronological while the narrative of time is not. Ricoeur employs Northrop Frye's expression, 'the narrative time that mediates between the episodic aspect and the configurational aspect' (1984: 67). Plot (re)configures chronological time into storied and teleological time. Emplotment grasps together configuration from mere succession. The synthesis can occur in the conclusion of a story where all the contingencies, factors and events are given a point of view and formed into a whole understanding. We learn how

the events, factors and episodes lead to a foregone and irreversible conclusion. To know or follow a story is to be able to recognize episodes as familiar and to know how these lead to the inevitable ending.

Mimesis$_3$

Ricoeur says narrative 'has its full meaning when it is restored to the time of action and of suffering in mimesis$_3$' (1984: 700). In this third representative stage H.G. Gadamer's hermeneutics of 'application' of the triadic cycle of meaning is fulfilled in the three-dimensional intersection (or intertextuality) of text and reader and real action. He takes three steps in answering four questions (step one is in questions 1 and 2, step two in question 3):

1. **Do the three stages of mimesis represent a progression as they bridge time and narrative?** In the circle of mimesis the end point (temporality) leads back to (or anticipates) the starting points, our pre-understandings (semantic structure of action, resources for symbolization, or temporal character) across the mid-point (emplotment). There are three reasons the circle of mimesis can be thought of as a spiral passing the same starting point several times across different vectors:

   - In the violence of interpretative narration, we could conclude temporal-consonance and the nostalgia for order replace dissonance and disorder. But for Augustine our experience of time was not reduced to mere dissonance but is rather dialectic of discordant concordance. And Ricoeur adds that our fascination with the unformed (or the horror of chaos) in temporal experience is a feature of modernity (1984: 72). 'Emplotment is never the simple triumph of "order"' (1984: 73). Plots coordinate distention and intention, not a mere triumph of order, such as the reversal of order of apocalypse, a catastrophe that abolishes time (1984: 73). And a plot is one among many alternative plots. The discordance of our temporal experience can be revealed as just another literary artifact, an alternative plot.
   - A redundancy of interpretation is the second objection to the spiral of mimesis being just a vicious circle. 'Mimesis$_2$ would then only restore to mimesis$_3$ what it had taken from mimesis$_1$ since mimesis$_1$ would already be a work of mimesis$_3$' (Ricoeur, 1984: 74):

     1.) it can be argued symbolism (or symbolic mediations) already mediates all human experience of which narratives is one;
     2.) we can assert we do not have access to temporal experience outside stories others and we tell (1984: 74).
     3.) These are untold events, a weighty story. Ricoeur's (1984: 74) reply is the concept of 'prenarrative' events and the untold story of episodes in our lives where stories are (as yet) prenarrated or demanding to be told. The psychoanalyst for example constructs a more intelligible story (or

case history) out of bits and pieces of our lived (or repressed or untold) stories, dreams and episodes that clients then believe is constitutive of their identity. The judge, jury, attorneys and witnesses unravel the tangle of plots and background in the prehistory of an emergent story a defendant is caught up in (1984: 74–5). And attorneys get paid to make a lived story more obscure and ambiguous. This emergent story constructs the subject as entangled in untold or prenarrated stories.

2. **How do plots dynamically model experience?** 'Thus the hermeneutic circle of narrative and time never stops being reborn from the circle that the stages of mimesis form' (Ricoeur, 1984: 76). This occurs through the step of configuration (modelling), refiguration (poetics of metaphorization) and reading in the transition between mimesis$_2$ and mimesis$_3$. In reading emplotment is an aesthetic of reception, an act of configuration and refiguration, a grasping together of selective details of action into a whole in ways that transcend the binary of inside/outside text. We, for example, can follow a story line by placing it in the contexts of stories of comparable genre and the rules one expects of that paradigm. And the reader fills plays with the gaps and indeterminacies in the story by acts of configuration and refiguration. Reading joins mimesis$_2$ and mimesis$_3$.

3. **What are the difficulties of referentiality in the narrative order?** Defending against tautology and joining writing with reading is the first step. This question is the second step. I will use Kristeva's term of 'intertextuality' to label Ricoeur's second step. There are at least four areas of overlap between intertextuality and Ricoeur's answer to this question. The text is an 'open horizon' as it 'projects' situations of the reader and intersects many texts. This is Gadamer's (1960) 'fusion of horizons'. Like Kristeva, Ricoeur takes the sentence (or the word) as the unit of discourse within the system of signs. Texts are dialogues (co-references) with other texts (we have something to say) and anticipated readers (we may hear back). We may omit details of intertextual reference, but a reader can fill in the gaps and missing links (be extralinguistic) or not (invent referential illusion). And here intertextuality leaves the realm of positivism (and post-positivism), since we cannot observe the interweaving in metaphor and poetics. Like Kristeva, Ricoeur also has a focus on the internal interplay of the text and the fusion of the text's and the reader's horizons and the worlds that unfold and are remade beyond the text (1984: 79–80). Narrative through poetics (symbolic mediations) resignifies and reconfigures human action (or networks of intersignification), our pre-understanding of the world under mimesis$_1$ (1984: 81). And in our modernity moments we are oversignified with historical intentionality, totality and references to a real past, its untold story being rendered visible and empirical. But in the postmodern sense of Lyotard's

grand narrative, fiction borrows as much from history as history borrows from fiction (Ricoeur, 1984: 82). Again, as Kristeva and Ricoeur both note, there is an interweaving between history and narrative fiction.

4. **How much aid can a hermeneutic of narrated time expect from the phenomenology of time?** There is a pre-understanding of action in the symbolic mediations and in our practical temporality (Ricoeur, 1984: 83). Emplotment renders order (configuration and refiguration) to heterogeneous historical events, literary criticism (or poetics) and the phenomenology of time. Ricoeur seeks a purer phenomenology of time (the intuitive apprehension of the structure of time) than he finds in Augustine's aporetics and he cautions that one may not exist at all. Following Kant, he argues time is invisible, not to be observed. Yet certain augmentations can be made to Augustine's aporetics. He does this in a comparison of the hermeneutic circle with the circle of poetics of narrativity culminating in the problems of interweaving (intertextual) reference. If Augustine and Husserl's hermeneutics are subjectivist and dualize subject/object, then Heidegger's being-in-the-world (*Dasien*) in the ontology of Care is the first augmentation. But not quite, since Ricoeur returns to Augustine to discover just such an augmentation in the three-fold presence of temporal intervals. Or, said another way, time has both a quantitative and a qualitative epistemology. Yet Augustine's (and Husserl) and Heidegger's analysis of temporality diverge radically even though they pose analogous problems (being-within-time and being-towards-death). Where they differ radically is in the augment to the aporetic character of pure phenomenology. 'The paradox is that the aporia has to do precisely with the relations between the phenomenology of time and the human sciences – principally history, but also contemporary narratology' (Ricoeur, 1984: 86). For Ricoeur the relation between time and narrative is not only dialectic; it involves the mutual arrangement of hierarchies among the three-way conversation between history, literary criticism and phenomenology. He does this by relating the hermeneutic circle to the circle (or spiral) of the three stages of mimesis, and these inscribed in a dialectic of the poetics of narrative and aporetics of time (1984: 86). The radical divergence of Augustine and Heidegger is between time eternal transcending Apocalypse into everything (three-fold) present at the same time and the finitude of 'being-towards-death'. The three-in-one God or the god of time that is dead.

Implications and analysis

Followability

To be intelligible or followable the story proceeds from discourses that already have a narrative form or genre. It is the relation of narrative form (matrix of explanation), a changing situational context, and story followability through change by a reader that becomes of interest. From a antenarrative perspective, followability would vary in each situation. Ricoeur summarizes Gallie's (1968: 22) story definition:

> A story describes a sequence of actions and experiences done or undergone by a certain number of people, whether real or imaginary. These people are presented either in situations that change or as reacting to such change. In turn, these changes reveal hidden aspects of the situation and the people involved, and engender a new predicament which calls for thought, action, or both. This response to the new situation leads the story toward its conclusion. (1984: 150)

This definition of story and the concept of the followability of story allow us to look at narration as the emplotment of story, the construction of plot through pre-understanding and followability in the three stages.

Strategy and narrative
In the field of organization studies you see applications of the hermeneutic circle (for Ricoeur it is the circle or spiral of the three mimetic moments) in several articles. For example, Tojo Thatchenkery (1992) applies the hermeneutic circle to organizational change, and Barry and Elmes have applied the concept of narrative plot to organizational strategy: 'Accordingly, a narrative approach can make the political economies of strategy more visible (cf. Boje, 1996): Who gets to write and read strategy? How are reading and writing linked to power? Who is marginalized in the writing/reading process?' (1997: 430).

Ricoeur (1984) like Kristeva (see intertextuality, sections above) brings the readers and writers of narrative plot together. To think of organizational change and strategy implementation as part of the writing and reading of an organizational plot is a recent step being taken in organizational studies. The value of looking to Ricoeur and to hermeneutics is that it puts the process of writing and reading plot into a dynamic and poly-voiced context. 'A story the strategist tells is but one of many competing alternatives woven from a vast array of possible characterizations, plot lines, and themes' (Barry and Elmes, 1997: 433). Boje (1991) looks at how executives, customers and vendors use narrative devices (i.e. terse tellings, filling in the story blanks, glossing).

An example for office supply narration

The storytelling about strategy and change bridges the first and second stages of mimesis. I will outline the basics of a narrative analysis that follow the triadic model of mimesis developed by Ricoeur. As an example I chose text from my 1991 article on the Office Supply Company (Boje, 1991). I spent the better part of 1989 trailing around members of Goldco Office Supply Company (fictitious name) with a tape recorder. I transcribed my tapes and made more expanded field notes. As part of the study I did semi-structured interviews with the executives and managers of home and several branch offices, taped office and sales meetings, and hallway conversation, and conducted focus groups with a sample of customers and vendors. I kept the recorder running unless someone asked for something to be 'off the record'. Here is tape one of four of a strategy meeting held with the CEO, two consultants (I am one of these) and various managers that come in and out of the sessions.

In the transcripts stories are a constant part of the banter. Storytelling occurs as a tapestry as an inter-stitching of information among customers, managers, executives, vendors, employees and consultants. There is a series of stories told by each in meetings, focus groups, interviews, meetings, at meals and in face-to-face and phone conferences. The people in Goldco are plugged into what is happening in their industry, such as Boise and their local competitor Eastman. The stories help shape strategy and help in getting others on board as they consensually validate each other's apprehensions of ongoing experience. Office supply has its own special oral history, crafted in an ongoing process that is taken-for-granted. The stock of experiences is shared through narration, with stories crafted out of a continuous stream of experience (Schutz, 1967: 55–6). Only some acts, experiences and episodes get abstracted out of a continuous stream of experience and rendered as story or 'reconstructive reflection' (Schutz, 1967: 62–3). In these storytelling reflections, experiences are apprehended, distinguished, brought into relief and marked out from one another. The transcripts give us a view of the lay analysis of ongoing experience through collective storytelling. Schutz calls it a 'retrospective glance' (1967: 63).

What Ricoeur calls 'preunderstanding' or mimesis$_1$, or Schutz calls the 'stock of knowledge at hand', serves as a 'scheme of interpretation of his past and present experience, and also determines his anticipations of things to come' (Schutz, 1967: 74). This is analogous to Ricoeur's use of Augustine's 'three-fold presence' of time. The stories of experience constitute a sifting of the stock of shared knowledge of the office supply industry. Industry participants share stories that are similar in kind to the experiences they are storying and restorying. This story 'X' is the same type as that story 'Y'. What is interesting is that this is a mimetic activity they are doing naturally and it is one that I am attempting to participate in as an outsider (or limited participant observer). My participant role is as a consultant, someone who is employed by the CEO and by Goldco. As I participate longer in the setting I come to know more of the references being made in the stock of office supply industry knowledge at hand. As such the text is my study of their schemes of interpretation of emergent industry experiences. Given the level of volatile change there are many emergent experiences.

We have conducted interviews with each branch and headquarter manager and are now meeting to discuss how we will process customer and vendor focus group tapes with the executive committee (of upper managers), develop our strategy and respond to a company that has recently acquired Goldco along with several other regional office supply companies across the US. The Hanson group is requesting detailed budget reports in preparation to sell off its office supply firms to a third party. In a visit the Hanson executives found discrepancies in the compensations being paid out to sales people.

An example of emplotment (the second mimesis) can be seen in the office supply study. I looked at how collective acts of storytelling brought about a patterning of experiences – e.g. a pattern is no longer financially sound, or ethical, or it is still going on, etc. For example, 'The CEO and several vice presidents participate in a strategic planning session during which Harmon asks a question to which Doug [the CEO] reconstructs a story line (341–3) and then once again invites Sam to gloss one aspect of the story (lines 338–9) [numbers refer to lines in the story below]' (Boje, 1991: 117–18).

Printing was a different story

Harmon:	But is that the most effective way	335
	to do it? Do they hit the same places?	336
Doug:	Historically, in reading a little	337
	bit of the history and maybe Sam	338
	can help us out here. The printing	339
	business that we were writing was	340
	significant at one time and when the	341
	folks left for Epsilon they took that	342
	business with them and now we're going	343
	through a whole retraining process	344
Sam:	Well that could be so I mean	345
	printing again falls with the	346
	salesmen. A lot of the salesmen will	347
	not sell printing because they are	348
	afraid that the printing department,	349
	as in the past, has fouled up.	350
Kora:	Vickie has been wonderful.	351
Sam:	Yes I think Vickie has been	352
	wonderful. It is a matter of	353
	confidence in whoever it is there.	354
Ruth:	And I think training comes in here.	355
Jim:	When I was in sales I sold what I	356
	understood. If I didn't understand	357

Storytelling then is a way of drawing parallels between various patterns of experience or what Ricoeur calls 'networks of action' in mimesis$_1$. How people come together to make sense of context in storytelling brings us into the hermeneutic circle that bridges three mimetic moments. Ricoeur argues that readers cannot follow a story plot through its twists, turns, contingencies, coincidences and dead ends to a foregone narrative conclusion without a great deal of pre-understanding and that followability can be analysed in a structural model inter-relating time and narrative coherence. The model relates not just story, but history and narrative structure together, such as the 'unification or the disintegration of an empire', 'the rise or fall of a class, a social movement, a religious sect, or a literary style' (1984: 151). These are narratives of projects defining trends, patterns or themes in human thought, action and strings of contingent institutional events that require competencies to follow the contours of such stories. And our competencies to follow a story are also governed by our interests, sympathies, prejudices and expectations (1984: 152). So our pre-understandings (competencies and prejudices) are a precursor to our ability to follow the plot of a story, and finally our ability to fill in all the gaps and discontinuities with our understanding of layers of context. This interplay of (1) pre-understanding, (2) plot and (3) embedded contextuality constitutes Ricoeur's triadic model.

Conclusion

Organization, managerial and capitalism narratives and stories can be analysed for pre-understanding, emplotment and embedded contextuality. Ricoeur's emplotment takes us beyond the simplistic and positivist definition of a plot as the chaining of cause and effect or stimulus and response into a pattern/structure/arrangement/network bridging pre-understanding and context. In emplotment, the spiral of these three mimetic moments comes into play bringing with it the intertextuality of reader and writer, text and world, individual and collective.

In emplotment, the plot is not just a chronology of events or the schematic of a causal chain that links events and episodes together into a narrative structure. Emplotment is also the intertextual *arrangement* of events within the text, and the epistemology of time and being-within-time. As such plot is an extension of the causal assertion analysis of Chapter 6, but at a more grand level of narrative analysis. Emplotment is more than the structure of events within a story and the symbolic mediation of inscribed cause–effect chains of relationship among events and characters.

We find less rigorous definitions of plot in many places:

> The sequence of 'motivated' or causally related events or actions that make up the fictional narrative. Plot is typically structured on change or development of character or situation over time, and usually requires some sort of conflict. When we refer to plot, we generally refer to the way in which the story is told, its structure (e.g. including flashes back and forward, repetition, etc.).

The sequence of action – mystery, suspense, situations, events, turning points, the unfolding drama – is the plot, but the plot is not all there is to emplotment. Plot forms a structural basis for analysis of the parts of a story (context, character, journey, climax, resolution, etc.), but it is a narrow and reductionist analysis. To focus only on plot takes us down a linear pathway in our analysis. A linear narrative structure might include point of attack, exposition, inciting incident, rising action, discovery, complication, crisis, climax and resolution. But linear plot is only one emplotment. The structural time devices of narrative are not always linear and may include flashback, flash-forward, repetition and ellipsis.

8

Theme analysis

It is the *excess* and *in-between* of theme analysis that concerns us here. Ours is an antenarrative approach to theme analysis defining moves in-between and outside taxonomic classification. Taxonomy cells in narrative theory are little theme cages to entrap stories. Antenarrative aims not to be caged in taxonomy or the hierarchy of classification. An antenarrative analysis highlights the storytelling moves and flows beyond narrative theme limits. Theme analysis without antenarrative would divest story of time, place, plurality and connectivity.

Theme and taxonomy from an antenarrative view is a terrorist discourse, an analysis reduced to stereotypes. Narrative degrades storytelling replacing it with new plots and more cohesion than inheres in the field of action. Narrative theme analysis is a foreclosure on storytelling polysemy and a debasement of living exchange. Beyond the cells of taxonomy is the messy plenitude. Antenarrative theme analysis steps outside containment to engage fragmentation, becoming and undoing. It is appropriate as our last chapter, since it involves all that we have done and undone thus far. First, I will examine theme analysis in depth. This will include a closer look at deductive, inductive and emic (insider categories) and etic (outsider) categories. Secondly, I will attempt to go beyond theme analysis by taking an antenarrative approach. I will do this in the context of a brief field example where I start with a theme and sub-theme analysis of narrative types and move on to an antenarrative analysis.

What is theme analysis?

Theme analysis is a respected and well-established and widely-used method of qualitative analysis (see Spradley, 1980). There is a mix of deductive and inductive, etic and emic in theme analysis.

Deductive theme analysis

A deductive approach collects stories like marbles and sorts them by their colours, sizes and stripes into 'etic' taxonomy. 'Etic' refers to the categories of the analyst drawn from grand theory and imposed from the outsider viewpoint onto others' worlds. Spradley (1980), for example, gives step-by-step deductive analysis methods to use to search transcripts and field notes for cultural themes. These themes are emic categories in use by insiders that come to be internalized by the ethnographer, living in the field. For example, in a study of a Choral Company (CC), we (Boje et al., 1999) analysed several narrative themes:

- how the CC stories were polyphonic;
- how each story has important ownership rights;
- how storytellers and story-listeners co-construct and collectively shape the telling of CC stories; and
- how the CC and the researchers are complicit in stories that will be told for years to come at our respective institutions, whereas the academy audience, the manuscript reviewers, and you the article reader, all become part of the co-construction of these stories.

Inductive theme analysis
Narrative themes are among the cultural themes that for Spradley (1980) emerge from systematic examination of transcripts and observations. Narrative themes can be imposed from some etic (outsider deductive theory) or developed with ethnographic professional sensitivity to emic (insider inductive or grounded situational usage). The inductive approach to narrative theme analysis apes its taxonomy from the emic categories in use by people who tell stories. Emic is how insiders sort their stories. And grounded theory, it is said, moves between etic and emic, with an eye on refining their alignment through successive comparison. Theme analysis, be it deductive, inductive or grounded, divests story of contextual markers in order to make maps.

For example, Spradley says, 'analysis is a search for *patterns*' and that a 'componential analysis can be used to search text for 'systematic units of cultural meaning' (1980: 85, 130–1). The componential analysis has several steps (Spradley, 1980: 133–9):

1. **Select a domain for analysis.** In this example we have selected a taxonomy of four types of narrative (see Table 8.1): bureaucratic, quest, chaos and postmodern.
2. **Inventory all contrasts previously discovered.** We identified contrast questions that compared the various themes during our analysis of transcripts in the first phase of the study. Any statement in the transcripts that compared one type of organizing narrative with another was given special scrutiny.
3. **Prepare a paradigm worksheet.** 'A paradigm worksheet consists of an empty paradigm in which you enter the cultural categories of the domain down the left hand column' (Spradley, 1980: 135). In the paradigm worksheet the idea is to compose questions that compare and contrast the four types. We will not be doing this.
4. **Identify dimensions of contrast that have binary values.** A contrast has two or more categories, and answers a question for the analyst

Table 8.1   *Basic narrative themes*

Key • Etic ♦ Emic ❖ Both ➢ Antenarrative	**Monophonic narrative** ←- - - - - - - - - - - - - - - -→ **Polyphonic narrative**	
Scientific knowledge narrative ↑ ⋮ ⋮ ⋮ ⋮ ⋮ ⋮ ⋮ ⋮ ⋮ ↓	**BUREAUCRATIC** ❖ Hierarchy ♦ Red tape • Functional ♦ Stuck in tradition	**CHAOS** ❖ Chaos (emic/etic) • Complexity ❖ Adaptive systems ❖ Edge of chaos
	ANTENARRATIVE ➢ Between the boxes ➢ Flows between cells ➢ Intertextual ➢ Polysemous ➢ Multi-layered and embedded ➢ Story networking behaviours ➢ Excess not in this taxonomy	
Aesthetic knowledge narrative	**QUEST** • Call (individual/organization) • Journey (individual/organization) • Return (individual/organization) ❖ Reorganization adventures	**POSTMODERN** • Post-industrial • Post-Fordist • Postmodern

such as 'what are the types of organizational narrative?'. We could also ask, 'what are the types of etic approaches to the four narratives?'.

5. **Collapse closely related dimensions of contrast.** Some of the binary contrasts among the types can prove to be related and therefore be collapsed. If there is no difference between chaos and postmodern, then collapsing is appropriate (but of course there are).

6. **Prepare contrast questions for missing attributes.** We can identify from the paradigm contrasts, the kinds of information we have to collect in the next round of interviews. This ensures we are being systematic.

7. **Conduct selective observations to discover missing information.** Continue to search for additional narratives and for important contrasts among, for example, the various narrative types in Table 8.1.

8. **Prepare a completed paradigm.** The paradigm we developed after repeated visits and focus groups became the layout displayed in Table 8.1. We built worksheets and NUD*IST (software) retrieval programs that would track the location of various quotes to each of the themes in Table 8.1.

Once a taxonomy of themes and their component contrasts (dimensions of similarity and difference) has been erected, then the researcher steps back to look at the overall 'paradigm' chart (Spradley, 1980: 132). The themes and sub-themes are neatly packaged by the taxonomy, and only publication remains.

What if we continue on?
An antenarrative approach to theme analysis is about what gets left out of the themes and taxonomy cages and what goes on between cells. What is beyond the map? Recall that for Peirce, abduction allowed for speculation between the poles of deductive and inductive method. Beyond the themes is the discovery of the web of '*in situ*' stories people tell one another to make sense of their unfolding experience. This would be a theme analysis about their speculation – theme hunches about theme. Also beyond the map is the interplay between outsider and insider; the stories not admitted to the cell.

Narrative mapmaking robs story of time, place, plurality and connectivity. Narrative theme analysis stops storytelling in its tracks; it arrests it. In organizations, I assume all storytellers are not created equal. Some storytellers by virtue of hierarchical position, personality and experience are able to speak while others live out a narrative existence in silence. Their emic categories are more likely to be netted by the expert analyst and become thematic abstract. These naïve storytellers get to narrate, but the expert (etic) categories cannot hear.

The purpose is to unfold an antenarrative theme analysis that is sensitive to antenarrative storytelling dynamics, how storytellers use their stories at work as well as to issues of etic and emic coding. Otherwise, narrative theme analysis degrades storytelling, the behaviour of the folk and the way they tell stories gets replaced by causal maps, themes and taxonomic charts, suitable for overhead display.

Stories in some studies are collected, stacked, bundled and counted; then placed in theme taxonomies. But, for me, there is interiority to stories where the inner folds refold and unveil to open up the storytelling economy. Derrida might enter this discussion and say that *the story has not given up its 'fold' to another discourse.* Antenarrative stories can put the institution into question. I had spent about eight months carrying a tape recorder around an office supply firm (Boje, 1991), taping everything. I wanted to see how stories were performed in organizations. I taped hallway conversations, meetings, hotel strategy sessions, conversations in the car, and what I couldn't tape I put into field notes. They thought I had some kind of taping fetish. I would transcribe the tapes each week for eight months and look for the stories. The conversation that seemed to have no story was actually a thread of an interweaving story line, a phenomenon that blurred the distinction between story and conversation. As I followed the threads, interesting story lines were traced. The stories unfolded and refolded themselves in snippets across hundreds of pages of narrative. As one CEO replaced another, and another, the vendors and the salespeople had to make new deals with each new administration – sort of like our White House. With all the changes, the story about Goldco was that 'it was kind of a ship without a rudder' (Boje, 1991: 121).

Stories are exemplars of the messy process of human sensemaking. For Derrida (1991), everything important is in the margins or traces. The trace is a clue (a footprint) and in it is hidden in the story. No story, for example, begins from a beginning to an end; at most it pretends to come back and to unfold, but does not exactly trace or replicate the original telling. A story may be only the possibility of meaning, what the past has promised the present. Storytelling is a dialogue across the veil. As Derrida puts it: 'Each includes the other, comprehends the other, which is to say that neither comprehends the other' (1991: 267). He continues:

> Each 'story' (and each occurrence of the word 'story,' each 'story' in the story) is part of the other, makes the other a part (of itself), each 'story' is at once larger and smaller than itself, includes itself without including (or comprehending) itself, identifies itself with itself even as it remains utterly different from its homonym. (Derrida, 1991: 267)

The tellers and inquisitors are picking fragments of stories to tell and to gloss in the story performances in organizational contexts. The story is woven into, out of and across turn-by-turn conversation.

I am arguing here against taxonomy and instead looking to trace stories, to see how story themes are embedded contextually in folds and refolds. The following example blurs any boundary between female metaphor and the sexual context of the account.

The couch story   Doug told me this story:

> I was here around 2 A.M. to visit the night crew. I had met just about everyone else in the company. After talking a bit with the guys on the loading dock, I went to my office. As I approached I saw the light on. Then, as I came closer I could hear someone in my inner office. As I looked through the outer door, I saw pants, and shorts and shoes all about the floor. I passed the secretary's office and opened my office door very quietly and very slowly. There on my new leather couch was my Vice President of Marketing and one of our best sales reps going at it. They were embarrassed. I was embarrassed. I said something like 'oh excuse me,' and waited for them to get dressed.
>   What would you have done at this point? What is your recommendation? I (Boje) told Doug that given what he had told me about the VP's excessive drinking and the embarrassing exchange at the party for their key corporate accounts, it was time to cut this guy loose.
>   Doug agreed: 'I asked him to write a letter of resignation.' Now what do I do about the girl? Do I fire her too? Do I listen to her side? Perhaps, she is the victim? Are they in love? She is our best sales rep. If she goes, some of our key accounts go with her. Our competition would love that. I told Doug, 'I would hear her side and see what were the circumstances.' That is what I did. I decided who she slept with was her business, but not on my couch. 'Am I fired?' she asked. I told her she was not fired. I did not have to say much, she was thoroughly embarrassed.

The marketing executive and the sales account manager were doing a private sexual act. It was private until Doug came in. Then it was public and potentially very public. This was no footprint of a sex act. This was the act in full view. Doug saw his meaning as CEO and as the rightful owner of the couch. We can fill in many blanks. Doug spent tens of thousands of dollars on his office furniture. As Dilbert, the cartoonist, tells us, 'office supplies are more important to managers than people.'

The 'couch story' is related to other stories of how salesmen and saleswomen had been lured or seduced by competitors and took very valued accounts with them. The institution relies on personal relations between sales people and the account people. Doug was installed by the holding company to 'rationalize' and institutionalize the 'personal'.

There is also tactical ambiguity. The couch story had to be hidden in a 'cover story'. The other workers were told 'the VP of marketing has resigned to take a new job.' Would the story leak? Would 'the word be on the street'?

Etic, emic circularity

Herein lies the breakdown of the etic/emic duality. Each is the other: emic becomes etic; etic becomes emic; they are in circularity. The etic researcher appropriates the emic category, publishes the theme analysis and taxonomy, and then some applied journalist writes a piece that is accessible to the masses. The next researcher comes to the field and discovers categories in use that were once emic, became etic, and are now emic once more. For a theme analysis, I propose to study the etic/emic process and the interplay of narrative and antenarrative processes. In our brief example I will look at a several theories of organization and how people experience each. Filling in the blanks is an interesting area. If I say to you, 'you know the story' then I am relying upon you to tell yourself the untold aspects of plot, characters, morality, context, ownership rights and implication. The full meaning of the story, if there is one or if one is even possible, requires me to explore the referents that extend beyond the story. The story is intertextual. It is networked or latticed across and between the telling and the organization.

Science lab theme analysis

We are now analysing a Southwestern science laboratory (hereafter 'Science Lab') and coding interview, meeting tapes and field notes for emergent and imposed (e.g. by the top) narrative themes. There are a little over two hundred full-time employees and administrators at Science Lab and another hundred doing part-timework and assignments at remote sites. Our qualitative methods seminar (eight students) was asked to study the organization redesign already under way. In our semi-structured interviews we asked very few questions and invited the interviewees to narrate. We asked open-ended questions about the history of Science Lab, its current transitions and its future. We also asked them to draw for us the web of communication and work arrangements among the various units and teams in the lab. Since we had four interview teams and eight people doing transcription, we developed early agreement on coding procedures:

Coding key

/ = A run-on sentence without pause or overlapping dialog.
(1, 2, 3, etc.) Seconds of silence or pause.
'.' Periods are placed where there is a pause between phrases.
',' Inserted in sentences for clarity
' ' Single quote marks indicate that a person is quoting another person or even themselves in a recounted conversation.
(?) Cannot make out preceding exact word.
(tr) Voice trails off so low that it is a whisper between two (tr)s.
CAPS/Bold – these are words that are said more loudly and emphatically than utterances either before or after.
Uhhh or similar sounds in bold letters are assumed to have significant meaning. The more 'hhh's the longer the sound.
Paragraphs – Paragraphs are set off by shifts in topic or theme.
{ANALYSIS NOTE: … } This is a note by David on parts that seem promising for various further follow-up work or reflection.

The Science Lab director wanted to de-bureaucratize and transform Science Lab (SL) into what the director calls an 'edge of chaos' organization. He also described how the organization was resisting efforts to be transformed into an 'edge of chaos' organization:

So **hahhhh** one thing that has happened though in the organization is (2) I've moved the organization where/and I'm a believer in the edge of chaos type of approach to an organization. But the people are very traditional (2.5) **uhhh** individuals that/in particular when you go through a downsizing what that means is over the course of roughly ten years which is roughly the period that SL didn't grow or downsized. (3) You don't have new people very few new people so you've got a clump of people that are way out here and you don't really have anything else. So you've got a culture that's really bound.

But there's that pressure. **People DO NOT LIKE** to work in an organization that has edge of chaos. I've had uhh people that uhh will come to you and say 'I just don't know what's going on any more. I just uhh before I knew what I was supposed to do. What was going on.' Of course what they knew to do was not the things we needed done./

Our research question was to understand the meaning of design and redesign and such constructs as 'edge of chaos' to the participants of Science Lab. We agreed to conduct 22 semi-structured interviews that we would tape, transcribe and analyse as input to three focus groups and a debriefing we would conduct. In this debriefing we report on the emic (insider = bottom up narrative frames) and etic (outsider = our own narrative frames and those at the top of Science Lab). We also crafted and launched an on-line web survey in which people could write in open-ended responses (anonymity was an option) to questions about 'chaos' and three other forms we found in our initial interviews and meetings. We wanted a chart that had both. Such a chart is presented in Table 8.1. Over the course of a semester-long study, the narrative content categories seemed, to us, to capture a complex web of themes and counter-themes.

Table 8.1 is a simple display of four narrative types and their respective dimensions of contrast. But here we put a wrinkle in the taxonomy by including how people experience the emic categories, borrowed from etic categories of chaos theory, bureaucratic, postmodern and quest. In this analysis are etic, emic-negative and emic-positive. The dimensions of the theme analysis are two contrasts: monophonic versus polyphonic (horizontal dimension) and scientific versus aesthetic knowledge (vertical dimension). A monophonic narrative has a single voice, its plot is evident, and there is a high level of coherence to the narrative. Bureaucratic narratives about traditions at Science Lab and its red tape were emic categories (language in use), while functional division of labour was an etic category taken from Weber. In the case of 'hierarchy' both the Science Lab members and Weber spoke about it. Table 8.1 has a key to indicate which categories were emic, etic or both. Both chaos and postmodern were considered more multivariate narratives than either bureaucratic or quest. By multivariate we mean differing along several dimensions, such as monophonic/polyphonic, centred/de-centred, linear/non-linear, coherent/fragmented emplotment, etc.

The second dimension refers to two types of knowledge: scientific and aesthetic. Bureaucracy and chaos/complexity are the new and old sciences of complex organization.

Bureaucratic narrative type

In the old science, strict division of labour and well-defined tasks with a hierarchy of supervision was by Henri Fayol's time seen as scientific administration while time and motion studies applied to work and job design were the stuff of Taylor's scientific management. Max Weber's bureaucratic ideal type was supposed to correct the deficiencies of pre-modern feudal and charismatic authority structures. And all bureaucracies claim up and down, 'we are not a pyramid' or that 'the hierarchy is being flattened' or otherwise reformed.

Science Lab was no different in this respect. Professionalization and the division of labour were considered acts of progress for Weber, resulting in more efficient orders. But as Weber (1958) notes at the end of the *Protestant Ethic*, the iron cage of rationality has its own dysfunctions. One dysfunction is what Ritzer (2000) terms the 'irrationality of rationality'. The manager participates in bureaucratic processes that render story lines predictable; life is always getting better through successive reforms in administrative process, be they TQM, re-engineering or knowledge organization transformations.

But if one peels back the narratives of rationality, there is a swarm of 'vulnerability, futility, and impotence' (Frank, 1995: 97). And not much is getting better, in the emic experience of Science Lab employees. This can mean that story lines of coherent sequences of events told in the official and proper narrative (at the top) do not adequately reflect the lived irrational experience of customers and workers. For bureaucracy chaos is the enemy, something to control and eliminate. But not everyone wanted to remove bureaucratic control and get too close to chaos or postmodern.

Chaos narrative type
The new science is not bureaucracy, it is chaos and complexity, and its advocates favour flexibility of control, a looser structure, and embedding self-organizing units in a more dynamic system than bureaucracy. We looked at chaos as science knowledge in its etic application, but also as anxiety over feeling/being out of control (in its emic expression). The lay experience of chaos can be one of the pits of disorder and an abyss of anxiety. As Letiche (2000) argues the phenomenal experience of chaos differs from the (etic) science metaphors of Stuart Kauffman and Ilya Prigogine. To deny the lay experience of chaos is an act of reductionism and exclusion, an imposition of the deductive (etic) category onto existential experience. It is not clear that living in chaos is less anxiety provoking than the iron cage of bureaucracy.

But to the scientist (the definer of etic categories) chaos has dissipative and more entropic aspects, and systems move in and out of chaos patterns. And if you can skate along the edge of the abyss there are efficiencies and profitable adaptive performances there. The Director of Science Lab has read of the 'edge of chaos' form of organization and sought to implement it.

The science of chaos and complexity is being increasingly applied to organization. For example, Margaret Wheatley's book (1992) contends that concepts such as 'fractals', 'strange attractors' and 'edge of chaos' can be applied to leadership and design in ways that dislodge traditional systems thinking. Peter Senge, Tom Peters and others are popularizing chaos organization as an alternative to the bureaucratic science of (mechanistic systems) management. As such chaos has concepts such as 'edge of chaos' and 'adaptive systems' that have moved into popular usage and have become both emic and etic.

Quest narrative type

We looked at quest in the Joseph Campbell sense of (1) receiving a call, (2) embarking on a journey of discovery, and (3) returning with the elixir or 'boon' that transformed the individual and/or the community (in this case Science Lab). This pattern is said by Campbell to be a universalized archetype for people widely separated in time and place. We classified 'quest' as a type of narrating that was more aesthetic than scientific (re-engineers and information science consultants may disagree). We also saw quest as a more monologic structure with one story to tell and a casting of characters in coherent roles.

In the quest narrative, for example, the hero of the journey has a story to tell. There is first a call to adventure, and after some false starts and meeting and recruiting companions, the hero departs on the journey. The hero of the tale is overwhelmed by life and takes off on a journey where more overwhelming events unfold. This threshold of departure crossed, the journey begins with some act of initiation that involves a series of trials. These usually mold the journey mob into a mighty team. Along the journey, the hero can be tempted and even atone for transgressions. At the end of the journey, the hero is transformed, returning not only with the loot, but also with values that have been transformed.

Narratively, the journey experiences are organized in the telling to be both coherent and meaningful and can be the dominant theme of strategy (Barry and Elmes, 1997). Quest advances the hero theme, usually the strong CEO and managers who lead the organization to seize opportunities and overcome its threats and weaknesses (i.e. SWOT strategic narratives). Other strategic narratives are classified by Barry and Elmes as more 'technofuturist', a definite possibility for Science Lab.

Quests can be a positive experience for their initiators but a negative one for those who must endure the quest. These are etic categories in Table 8.1, but one could argue as well that they are widely accepted and popular archetypes, available to anyone who has seen 'Star Wars' movies. We could argue that since they are so widely available 'call', 'journey' and 'return' (used in almost all movie plots) are emic popular culture categories. But no one at Science Lab used the words 'quest', 'journey', 'call', or 'return'. However, they did speak of historical episodes and going through organizational transformations, some with valued results, and others, such as downsizing episodes, were shocks to everyone. We were not the first researchers/consultants at Science Lab. Finally, there was significant concern among the eight qualitative researchers that the Director's embrace of 'edge of chaos' theory was itself a type of quest; some favoured loosening up of the system, while others did not. Since he is an insider that could be grounds for making his 'call' emic.

Postmodern narrative type

Postmodern narrative was classified as more aesthetic and polyphonic. Best and Kellner (1997) describe postmodern as a turn toward a different aesthetic. They also look at postmodern as a science, different from the mechanistic sciences of Newton. However, in looking at the postmodern sciences what gets mentioned is complexity and chaos.

For Frank (1995: 137–40) a postmodern narrative is testimony in which fragments of some larger whole are told by an individual witness who 'makes no pretense of grasping in [sic] its entirety'. This fits well with the postmodern condition as the fragmentation of time and space as storytelling is about being overwhelmed by all the bits and pieces that are no longer coherent in grander narrative frameworks. The excess, the storytelling that does not fit the narrative frames, is part of both chaos and postmodern.

There is then a boundary issue between chaos and postmodern, an overlap and flow between. Postmodern narrative is not something people at Science Lab talked about. People did not speak of 'postmodern science' or 'aesthetics'. These were our 'etic' labels. They did talk of confusion, being overwhelmed and bewildered. But is this chaos or postmodern, or both?

But there are many definitions of postmodern. To some it is the post-industrial condition, to others it is fragmentation and the undoing of late modern. What Science Lab people did describe was a move from bureaucracy to a 'post-something' that is some type of hybrid of the types in Table 8.1. For example, a branch manager told us:

> Postmodern may actually be the best type, as far as technical support goes. Bureaucracy, to some extent, may be necessary to maintain an effective structure across the entire organization. Many of the technical groups, as a sub-organization, already fall under this type of structure by default. The group needs to function as a team with empowered members that can react to the challenges without having to work through management.

We therefore included concepts such as post-industrial, post-Fordist and late modern with our (etic) concerns for postmodern aesthetics. During the course of the study we came to look upon Science Lab as a hybrid form of organization, one composed of much bureaucracy, pockets of chaos organizing attempts, some former and current quests and postmodern 'something'.

In sum, we decided to focus the study on the interplay of these four forms and narrative frames in Table 8.1. The most frequently mentioned theme was bureaucratic, followed by 'quest' due to the attempts at reform to bureaucracy, and chaos; postmodern dimensions were the least mentioned. As Table 8.1 suggests, we were interested in differences between the (emic) existential experience of chaos versus some imposed (etic) theory of a chaos organization. What I want to do now is look at the case for ante-narrative analysis.

Antenarrative
At the centre of Table 8.1 is our focus on antenarrative. We sought to oppose our own taxonomic classification. We wanted to analyse what we were leaving out, what was the excess. And we wanted to focus on the intertextual, the relations between our cells, and between etic and emic

classification. We focused therefore on what was between the lines and boxes of our taxonomy. Where was chaos like postmodern? And we focused on what flowed between the cells. Some transcript examples, as the one above from the branch manager, seemed to contain all or most of the cells. We concluded that there were intertextual references between what we placed in the cells.

Our antenarrative focus was on the polysemous (i.e. rich in multiple meaning and interpretation). There is also a sense here that Science Lab has multiple layers with bits of narration that are embedded in other narrative types. This is what Barthes terms a 'chain of discourse, the progress (progressus) of discursivity' (1977: 200). Science Lab began in bureaucracy, a requirement for its many military contracts following World War II, but over time there was a succession of quests to change that form, and the most recent ones are chaos and bureaucracy. The chain, however, is a broken one, and instead of progress, there is only plurality and perhaps the fictive illusion of progress. It is not clear that chaos, for example, is a quantum leap over its predecessor.

NUD*IST (NVivo) computer software facilitated a cross-theme analysis of transcripts based upon etic and emic manifestations of the four types. Pairs of students in my qualitative methods seminar analysed 28 transcripts, each team focusing upon a particular narrative theme. I worked with the eight PhD students in the theme analysis, working independently and then together to reach consensus on differences in coding approaches. Once theme categories were agreed to, pairs of student-coders analysed transcripts of Science Lab interviews using these same themes.

Each theme, such as bureaucratic narrative, was coded for more specific themes, such as the etic (officially imposed theme) versus etic (emergent or bottom up themes). In our theme analysis, we found that while coding transcripts into themes and categories (called nodes in NUD*IST) was a systematic way to go, there was a good deal of information lost in this approach. That is, when a particular utterance was coded for software storage and retrieval, we lost the context of the remark. Our approach therefore was traditional, using full transcripts, highlighter pens (of various colours) and extensive margin notes. This allowed us to preserve the context of each utterance. The NUD*IST storage and retrieval became a supplement to our hand coding of themes.

As our complex web of themes developed, i.e. the battle between the edge of chaos and the traditional bureaucracy narrative, we returned to our key informants to dialogue about what we considered their emergent themes. In some cases the themes were confirmed and others not.

Based upon Table 8.1, the overall narrative theme became a comparison of the emic and etic narrative experience of the Science Lab participants. Our approach to theme analysis was to inventory the various narrative types, develop dimensions of contrasts and return to the filed to find out if our typology was meaningful to the participants. We also wanted to find out how each narrative type (i.e. bureaucratic, quest, chaos and postmodern) impacted the life space of the participants. How recurrent were the themes in their life space and how did the narratives control or limit behaviour?

While the componential analysis served to point out differences in our narrative typology, what it failed to do was look between the lines. We therefore analysed the transcripts to determine the ways in which chaos and bureaucratic, chaos and postmodern, bureaucratic and quest, quest and postmodern, etc. overlapped in significant ways. We wanted to see if participants had the experience of the lines being blurred between our types. Were we assuming narrative theme homogeneity and harmony when there was a good deal of blur? Further, it could well be that some themes, such as chaos, were restricted to particular units of Science Lab, while others such as bureaucratic cut across many units. We therefore returned to the transcripts and the site to ascertain in what contexts the four narrative themes were more or less manifest.

We must admit that we caused narration by our interrogation of Science Lab. The stories that we caused to be narrated circulated around Science Lab, including stories of our interviews and what we might be about. And our analysis as we met each week to share transcripts and coding ideas was a time to tell stories and to narrate Science Lab into our typology. In short there were intertextual and rhizomatic relations between types, and between us and them – all the excess that is unstated in this taxonomy.

Each narrative theme collected by the researcher becomes a one-sentence, often linear story that gets summarized into a label of one or several words, a 'theme'. Our typology is made up of stereotypes, theirs and ours. Such a linear narrative theme can be a simplistic, reductionist and oppressive way to give account for a complex and otherwise polyphonic storytelling organization. An antenarrative analysis is about the stuff left out of the label and the plenitude beyond the taxonomic arrested items. The question becomes how do we conduct an antenarrative theme analysis in ways that preserve the dynamic relation between an insider (emic) and outsider (etic) analysis and do not turn reductionistic and linear?

A linear narrative presents a theme that appears all too easy to analyse since the non-linear escapes accountability of multiple interpretation. The story is no longer polysemous when it is caged and reduced to thematic taxonomy.

Conclusions

It is the non-linear and fragmented narrative spaces that have been our focus in Chapter 8. A non-linear narrative does not present the coherent plot structure and there is the polyphony of storytellers to dispute the primacy of any one theme. And instead of etic or emic, our theme analysis is an act of co-construction (a compromise to polysemy) between their many stories, our demands that they narrate and our own narrations. Finally, each researcher came to the field with one (etic or outsider) theme while the participants have their own (emic or insider) existential narrative experience of some etic theme.

The narrative themes recur with varying regularity across time and space. In terms of time, the chaos and postmodern themes are the more recent ways of sensemaking than quest or by far the oldest, bureaucratic. As such across time and space there is a tension among the themes to dominate and absorb one another. Bureaucratic interprets etic narratives of chaos as interference in the smooth running machinery of Science Lab. The CEO's attempts at reform are interpreted, in several divisions, as a way to move forward, a quest that is emic-positive, but in other areas as a quest that is emic-negative, spinning Science Lab out of control and away from rationality.

In sum my analysis of narrative themes looked at the kinds of organizing narratives that construct the cultural space of Science Lab. I contrasted the various narratives by looking at the etic and emic experiences of these narratives. Finally, I examined the ways in which the narratives were more or less manifest across the time and space of Science Lab. And I looked at ways in which my four types blurred and imploded into one another into the web of narratives that construct the existential experience, collective memory and, I think, behaviour of Science Lab.

I want to assert that there was not one universal narrative theme that defined Science Lab. There was no grand narrative. There were narrative themes, such as bureaucratic and quest, that were more frequent. A chaos narrative is challenging the hegemony of the bureaucratic interoperation of experience and the ordering of appropriate and inappropriate behaviours. Science Lab is replete with the kinds of cultural contradictions that make for a postmodern narrative. There is fragmentation and the 'official' narrative is not a mediating theme for all of Science Lab. There are informal story networks that counter attempts to revise the bureaucratic narrative. There is also a sense of managing the narrative process, of attempting to supplant one narrative with others. This is part of the dynamics of Science Lab as a storytelling organization. Science Lab is in narrative flux: searching for a coherent narrative, but unable, as yet, to decide upon one.

I conclude that members of Science Lab are suspended in a complex web of storied relationships that change and move across time and space in resistance to opposing narratives. Some participants in the lab are able to make coherent sense of their experience in bureaucratic quest narratives. Others turn to the more incoherent and non-linear narratives of chaos and postmodern. Narrative theme analysis when done as more than a typology of dualized differences or etic narratives can reveal something of the complex storytelling dynamics of organizations.

Closing this book

As I wrap up this text on narrative and antenarrative methods, I want to reflect on the typology of the book. The eight analyses are laid out from deconstruction to theme, each posing narrative and antenarrative as a dialectic. Instead of destroying or usurping narrative analysis, the antenarrative analysis seems to me a supplement, a way to explore the gaps and excesses excluded in narrative analysis. There is intertextuality between the analyses.

Grand narrative and deconstruction are opposed by microstoria that contends there is a material text, and there is a resistance to grand narrative. Story networking continues the network of names begun in microstoria analysis, but the antenarrative contribution is to go beyond the architectural maps of networks. Intertextuality is itself a deconstruction of types and forms, a systems view of text, as an almost living organism, complete with interactions with textual fragments and references to more texts. Causality is the essence of plot, but emplotment challenges causality. Emplotment surrounds causality in the hermeneutic circle, and admits that where there is not sufficient pre-understanding or followability, there is antenarrative. I concluded with theme analysis by taking an antenarrative approach, and sought to swim between and outside the taxonomic cells.

I return full circle to the theme of the book, the juxtaposition of narrative and story. Narrative analysis (structuralism, semiotics, formalism) without antenarrative is the status degradation of story, an elitist act to make folklore subject to narratology. As Culler puts in his chapter, 'Story and Discourse in the Analysis of Narrative':

> There is considerable variety among these [narrative] traditions, and of course each theorist has concepts or categories of his own, but if these theorists agree on anything it is this: that the theory of narrative requires a distinction between what I shall call 'story' – a sequence of actions or events, conceived as independent of their manifestation in discourse – and what I shall call 'discourse,' the discursive presentation or narration of events. (Culler, 1981: 169–70)

Culler goes on to deconstruct the line between story as a sequence of events and narrative as the presentation of the interpretative plot and cohesion structure to the storied bits and pieces of chronology. Both narrative and stories report sequences (chronologies) of events, but with narrative there is effacement to the order and import of events by adding coherence. In this book, I have joined Culler in noting that there is a hierarchy functioning in the duality between narrative and story. There is a demand by narrative for 'causal efficacy' and a double logic, insisting on the 'primacy of events' while the others view 'events as the products of meanings' (Culler, 1980: 177–8). And here is the trap from which antenarrative derives its force: to look at storytelling where plot is not possible, where the sequence of events is chaotic and non-linear, and where there are competing claims for coherence (in polyphony and polysemy):

One could argue that every narrative operates according to this double logic, presenting its plot as a sequence of events which is prior to and independent of the given perspective on these events, and, at the same time, suggesting by its implicit claims to significance that these events are justified by their appropriateness to a thematic structure. (Culler, 1980: 178)

In storytelling there is the living exchange of story and prenarration, the ebb and flow that constitute the story networks and refuse to be contained in narrative analysis. And even to the call to fill into the appropriate cells in the thematic and taxonomic structure.

If there is a narrative space, then for me it is a fragmented one. One in which I have access to bits and pieces, to stories, but not to the total story or to some universal logic calling all the pieces to reassemble. I question the priority of narrative analysis over story and I see antenarrative as a way to resituate and rebalance the great divide and marginalization between narrative and story. Narratives stitch together stories of experiences that are sometimes best left fragmented. As such Culler observes and I agree 'narrative is an effect of self-deconstruction' (1980: 183). One approach to deconstruction, for example, is the 'reversal'; we reverse the notion that events are prior to their narration. That is to say, the narration makes the events come into discursive being. The narrative frame is self-deconstructing, vulnerable to every new story that unweaves the hierarchy, and each of the narrative analyses is self-deconstructing with each new one. This is my case for antenarrative.

References

Alvesson, Mats and Stanley Deetz (1996) 'Critical theory and postmodernism approaches to organizational studies.' In S.R. Clegg, C. Hardy and W.R. Nord (Eds.). pp. 191–217. *Handbook of Organization Studies*. London: Sage.

Alvesson, Mats and Hugh Willmott (1996) *Making Sense of Management: A Critical Introduction*. London: Sage.

Axelrod, R. (1976) 'The Analysis of Cognitive Maps,' in R. Axelrod (ed.) Structure of Decision: The Cognitive Maps of Political Elites, pp. 55–73. Princeton, NJ: University Press.

Bakhtin, M.M. (1986) Speech genres and other late essays. C. Emerson and M. Holquist (Eds., V.W. McGee, Trans.), Austin, TX: University of Texas Press.

Ballinger, Jeff and Claes Olsson (1997) *Behind the Swoosh: The Struggle of Indonesians Making Nike Shoes*. Sweden: Global Publicaitons Foundation.

Barry, David and Michael Elmes (1997) 'Strategy retold: Toward a narrative view of strategic discourse.' Academy of Management Review, 22(2): 429–452.

Barthes, Roland (1957) Mythologies. 1957 edition is Paris: du Seuil, 1970. Trans. 1972 by Jonathan Cape, Ltd. New York: The Noonday Press.

Barthes, Roland (1977) *Image MusicText*. Trans. Stephen Heath. New York: Hill and Wang, a division of Farrar, Straus and Giroux.

Bauman, Zygmunt (1989) *Modernity and the Holocaust*. Ithaca, New York: Cornell University Press.

Bauman, Zygmunt (1993) *Postmodern Ethics*. Oxford: Blackwell Publishers.

Bergson, Henri (1910) Time and Free Will: An Essay on the Immediate Data of Consciousness, translated by F.L. Pogson, M.A. London: George Allen and Unwin.

Best, Steven (1995) *The Politics of Historical Vision: Marx, Foucault, Habermas*. New York/London: The Guilford Press.

Best, Steven and Kellner, Douglas (1991) *Postmodern Theory: Critical Interrogations*. New York/London: The Guilford Press.

Best, Steven and Kellner, Douglas (1997) *The Postmodern Turn*. New York/London: The Guilford Press.

Boje, David M. (1991) 'Organizations as Storytelling Networks: A study of story performance in an office-supply firm,' *Administrative Science Quarterly*, 36: 106–126.

Boje, David M. (1995) 'Stories of the Storytelling Organization: A Postmodern Analysis of Disney as 'Tamara-land.' *Academy of Management Journal*, 38(4): 997–1035. See *http://cbae.nmsu.edu/~dboje/papers/DisneyTamaraland.html*

Boje, David M. (1998a) 'The Postmodern Turn form Stories-as-Objects to Stories-in-Context Methods.' Published in 1998 Academy of Management, Research Methods Forum #3, online – Robert Gephart, Editor. See *http://www.aom.pace.edu/rmd/1998_forum_postmodern_stories.html*

Boje, David M. (1998b) 'Amos Tuck's Post-Sweat Nike Spin' pp. 618–623. *In Business Research Yearbook: Global Business Perspectives*, Vol. V. Biberman, J. and Alkafarji, A. (Eds.).

Boje, David M. (1998c) 'Wile Coyote Meets the Road Runner' Paper presentation to the Sun Break Conference, Chaos and Complexity, chaired by Janice Black, Las Cruces, NM, February at New Mexico State University.

Boje, David M. (1998d) 'A Wicked Introduction to the Unbroken Circle' Conference: International Business & Ecology Boje, D.M. 1998. p. v–xiii. In *International Business and Ecology Research Yearbook*. A Publication of the International Academy of Business Disciplines. ISBN 1-889754-02-1.

Boje, David M. (1998e) 'How Critical Theory and Critical Pedagogy can Unmask Nike's Labor Practices' presented to the Critical Theory pre-conference of the Academy of Management meetings, San Diego, CA, August 8.

Boje, David M. (1998f) Nike, Greek 'Goddess of Victory or Cruelty? Women's Stories of Asian Factory Life.' *Journal of Organizational Change Management*. Vol. 11(6): 461–480.

Boje, David M. (1998g) 'What Postmodern Philosophers Have to Contribute to Knowledge Researchers' Paper presented to INFORMS (Institute for Operations Research and Management Sciences) conference, Seattle, WA, October.

Boje, David M. (1999) 'New Is Nike Roadrunner or Wile E. Coyote? A Postmodern Organization Analysis of Double Logic', *Journal of Business & Entrepreneurship*. Special Issue (March, Vol. II) 77–109.

Boje, David M. (2000a) 'Postmodern Organization Science: Narrative Ethics, Tamara and the Binary Machine.' Web document at *http://www.zianet.com/boje/tamara/papers/Boje_response_to_Weiss.html*

Boje, David M. (2000b) 'Corporate Imperialism Spectacle.' Chapter 3 of *Spectacles and Festivals: Managing production and consumption with Ahimsa*. Hampton Press. In press.

Boje, David M. (2000c) 'Nike Corporate Writing of Academic, Business, and Cultural Practices.' A shorter version will appear in *Management Communication Quarterly, Essays for the Popular Management Forum* Volume 14, Number 3.

Boje, David M. (2000d) 'Nike is Out of Time' – Introduction to the Time and Nike Showcase Symposium for Academy of Management Meetings – August, 2000 in Toronto.

Boje, David M. (2000e) 'Global Manufacturing and Taylorism Practices of Nike Corporation and its Subcontractors.' A research proposal to Nike Corporation and various associations. *http://cbae.nmsu.edu/~dboje/nike/call_for_nike_research.html*

Boje, D.M., Rosile, G., Dennehy, B. and Summers, D. (1997) 'Restorying reengineering: Some deconstructions and postmodern alternatives.' Accepted for publication in Special Issue on Throwaway Employees, *Journal of Communication Research*, 24(6): 631–668.

Boje, David M., John T. Luhman and Donald E. Baack (1999) 'Hegemonic stories and encounters between storytelling organizations.' *Journal of Management Inquiry*, 8(4): 340–360.

Boje, D.M., Alvarez Rossana C. and Schooling, Bruce (2000) 'Storytelling in organizational theory.' Chapter to appear in Stephen Linstead and Robert Westwood (Eds.) *Language and Organization*.

Braverman, Harry (1974) *Labor and Monopoly Capital: The Degradation of Work in the Twentieth Century*. New York: Monthly Review Press.

Brown, Richard Harvey (1991) 'Rhetoric, textuality, and the postmodern turn in sociological theory.' *Sociologicial Theory*, pp. 187–197.

Burrell, Gibson (1998) *Pandemonium: Towards a Retro-Organization Theory*. London: Sage.

Campbell, Joseph (1973) *The Hero with a Thousand Faces*. Princeton: Princeton University Press.

Chandler, A.D. (1964) *Strategy and structure*. Cambridge, MA: MIT Press.

Chandler, Daniel (1996) Semiotics for Beginners: Syntagmatic Analysis. Web document. *http://www.aber.ac.uk/~dgc/sem05.html*

Cilliers, Paul (1998) *Complexity and Postmodernism: Understanding Complex Systems*. New York/London: Sage.

Cixous, Hélène (1986) 'Sorties' in Cixous, H. and Catherine Clément (Eds.). *The Newly Born Woman*. Manchester: Manchester University Press.

Cixous, Hélène (1990) 'The Laugh Of The Medusa' in Walder, R. (ed.) *Literature In The Modern World*. Oxford: Oxford University Press.

Clair, Robin Patric (1998) *Organizing Silence: A World of Possibilities*. New York: State University of New York Press.

Clair, R.P., Chapman, P.A. and Kunkel, A.W. (1996) 'Narrative approaches to raising consciousness about sexual harassment: From research to pedagogy and back again.' *Journal of Applied Communication Research*. Vol. 24: 241–259.

Cook, T.D. and Campbell, D.T. (1979) *Quasi-experimentation*. Boston: Houghton Mifflin.

Coser, Lewis A. (1977) *Masters of Sociological Thought: Ideas in Historical and Social Context*, second edition. New York: Harcourt Brace Jovanovich.

Culler, Jonathan (1981) *The Pursuit of Signs: Semiotics, Literature, Deconstruction*. Ithaca, New York: Cornell University Press.

Currie, Mark (1998) *Postmodern Narrative Theory*. New York: St. Martin's Press.

Czarniawska, Barbara (1997) *Narrating the Organization: Dramas of Institutional Identity*. Chicago, IL: The University of Chicago Press.

Czarniawska, Barbara (1998) *A Narrative Approach to Organization Studies*. Qualitative Research Methods Series Volume 43. Thousand Oaks, CA: Sage Publications, Inc.

Deci, E.L. and Ryan, R.M. (1985a) 'The general causality orientations scale: Self-determination in personality.' *Journal of Research in Personality*, 19: 109–134.

Deci, E.L. and Ryan, R.M. (1985b) *Intrinsic motivation and self-determination in human behavior*. New York: Plenum.

Deleuze, Gilles and Felix Guattari (1987) *A Thousand Plateaus: Capitalism and Schizophrenia*, Trans. By Brian Massumi. Minneapolis: University of Minnesota Press.

Derrida, Jacques (1976) *Of Grammatology*. Baltimore, MD: Johns Hopkins University Press.

Derrida, Jacques (1977/1989) *Limited Inc abc*. Translated by Samuel Weber. 1977 is 1st edition. 1989 edition has an afterword to the debate with John Searle. Baltimore, MD: The Johns Hopkins University Press.

Derrida, Jacques (1991) 'Living on: Border lines.' In *A Derrida Reader: Between the Blinds* Peggy Kamuf (ed.). New York: Columbia University Press.

Derrida, Jacques (1994) *Specters of Marx, the state of the debt, the Work of Mourning, & the New International*, translated by Peggy Kamuf, London/New York: Routledge.

Derrida, Jacques (1999) 'Hospitality, justice and responsibility: A dialogue with Jacques Derrida.' pp. 65–83 in Kearney, Richard and Mark Dooley, *Questioning Ethics: Contemporary Debates in Philosophy*. London/New York: Routledge.

Fairclough Norman (1992) *Discourse and Social Change*. Cambridge: Polity.

Fairhurst, Gail T. and Putnam, Linda L. (1999) 'Reflections on the organizational-communication equivalency question: The contribution of James Taylor and his colleagues.' *The Communication Review*, Vol. 3(1–2): 1–19.

Fisher, Walter (1984) 'Narration as a human communication paradigm: The case of public moral argument.' Communication Monographs, 51: 1–22.

Fisher, Walter (1985a) 'The narrative paradigm: An elaboration.' *Communication Monographs*, 52: 347–367.

Fisher, Walter (1985b) 'The narrative paradigm: In the beginning.' *Journal of Communication*, 35: 75–89.

Flax, Jane (1990) *Thinking Fragments*. Berkley: University of California Press.

Follett, Mary Parker (1941) *Dynamic Administration: The Collected Papers of Mary Parker Follett*. Metcalf, H.C. and Urwick, L. (Eds.). New York: Harper & Bros.

Foucault, M. (1972) *The Archaeology of Knowledge*. New York: Pantheon Books.

Foucault, M. (1976) *Birth of The Clinic*. London: Tavistock.

Foucault, M. (1979) *Discipline and Punish*. Translated from the 1977 French by Alan Sheridan. New York: Vintage Books (Random House).

Frank, Arthur W. (1995) *The Wounded Storyteller: body, Illness, and Ethics*. Chicago: The University of Chicago Press.

Fraser, Donald (1999) *QSR NUD*IST Vivo: Reference Guide*. Melbourne, Australia: Qualitative Solutions and Research Pty. Ltd.

Fraser, Nancy and Linda Nicholson J. (1988) 'Social criticism without philosophy: An encounter between feminism and postmodernism.' *Theory, Culture and Society*, Vol. 5(2–3): 373–394.

Fraser, Nancy and Nicholson, Linda J. (1990) Social criticism without philosophy: An encounter between feminism and postmodernism. In L.J. Nicholson (ed.), Feminism/postmodernism. New York: Routledge.

Freeman, Linton C. (1999a) 'Using available graph theoretic or molecular modeling programs in social network analysis.' Nine page web document at *http://tarski.ss.uci.edu/new.html*

Freeman, Linton C. (1999b) 'Visualizing social networks.' Fourteen page web document at *http://carnap.ss.uci.edu/vis.html*

Freeman, Linton C. (1999c) 'Using molecular modeling software in social network analysis: A practicum.' Fourteen page web document at *http://electric.ss.uci.edu/~lin/chem.html*

Frye, Northrop (1957) *Anatomy of criticism; four essays*. Princeton, Princeton University Press.

Gadamer, H. (1960) *Truth and Method*. New York: Continuum.

Gallie, W.B. (1968) *Philosophy and the Historical Understanding*. New York: Schocken Books.

Game, A. (1991) *Undoing the Social*. Buckingham: Open University Press.

Gephart, Robert P., Jr. (1988) *Ethnostatistics: Qualitative foundations for quantitative research* (Qualitative Research Methods, Vol. 12). Newbury Park, CA: Sage.

Gephart, Robert P., Jr. (1993) 'The textual approach: Risk and blame in disaster sensemaking.' *Academy of Management Journal*, 36(2): 1465–1514.

Geertz, Clifford (1973) 'Thick description: Toward and interpretive theory of culture.' In C. Geertz, *The Interpretation of Cultures: Selected essays* (pp. 3–32). New York: Basic Books.

Geertz, Clifford (1988) *Works and lives: The anthropoligist as author*. Stanford, CA: Stanford University Press.

Ginzburg, Carlo (1980) *The Cheese and The Worms: The Cosmos of a Sixteenth-Century Miller*. Translated by John and Anne Tedeschi. Original in Italian 1976. English 1980. Baltimore/London: The Johns Hopkins University Press.

Glaser, Barney G. and Anselm L. Strauss (1967) *The Discovery of Grounded Theory: Strategies for Qualitative Research*. New York: Aldine Publishing Company.

Granovetter, M.S. (1973) 'The strength of weak ties.' *American Journal of Sociology*, 78: 1360–80.

Granovetter, M.S. (1985) 'Economic action and social structure: The problem of embeddedness.' *American Journal of Sociology*, 91(3): 481–510.

Harré, R. (1985) *The philosophy of science* (2nd ed.). Oxford: Oxford University Press.

Heidegger, Martin (1962) *Being and Time*. Trans. John Macquarrie and Edward Robinson. New York: Harper and Row.

Herndl, Carl (1993) 'Cultural studies and critical science.' In *Understanding Scientific Prose,'* ed. Jack Selzer. Madison: University of Wisconsin Press, pp. 61–81.

Huff, A. (1990) *Mapping Strategic Thought*. Chichester: Wiley.

Hutcheon, Linda (1989) *The Politics of Postmodernism*. London/New York: Routledge.

Illich, Ivan (1993) *In the Vineyard of the Text: A Commentary to Hugh's Didascalicon*. Chicago/London: The University of Chicago Press.

Irving, Washington (1828) *The Life and Voyages of Christopher Columbus*. New York: Clarke, Given & Hooper Publishers.

Iggers, Georg G. (1997) *Historiography in the Twentieth Century From Scientific Objectivity to the Postmodern Challenge*. Hanover/London: Wesleyan University Press (University Press of New England).

Jameson, Fredric (1984) 'Foreword' to *The Postmodern Condition*. Trans. By Geoff Bennington and Brian Massumi. Minneapolis: University of Minnesota Press.

Jameson, Fredric (1991) *Postmodernism, or, the Cultural Logic of Late Capitalism*. Durham, NC: Duke University Press.

Jarvis, Darryl S.L. (1998) 'Postmodernism: A critical typology.' *Politics & Society*, Vol. 26(1): 95–142.

Kamuf, Peggy (ed.) (1991) *A Derrida Reader: Between the Blinds*. New York: Columbia University Press.

Katz, Donald (1994) *Just Do It: the Nike Spirit in the Corporate World*. Holbrook, MA: Adams Publishing Co.

Kearney, Richard and Mark Dooley (1999) *Questioning Ethics: Contemporary Debates in Philosophy*. London/New York: Routledge.

Kilduff and Mehra (1997) 'Postmodernism and organizational research,' *Academy of Management Review*, 22: 453–481.

Klimecki, Ruediger and Lassleben, Hermann (1998) 'Modes of organizational learning: Indications from an empirical study.' *Management Learning*, 29(4): 405–430.

Kristeva, Julia (1980a) *Desire in Language: A Semiotic Approach to Literature and Art*. Edited by Léon Roudiez. Translated by Alice Jardine, Thomas Gora and Léon Roudiez. New York, Columbia University Press, London, Basil Blackwell.

Kristeva, Julia (1980b) 'Word, Dialogue, and Novel.' *Desire and Language*. Ed. Leon S. Roudiez. Trans. Thomas Gora et al. New York: Columbia UP, pp. 64–91.

Kristeva, Julia (1986) 'Word, dialogue, and the novel.' In T. Moi (ed.), *The Kristeva reader* (pp. 35–61). New York: Columbia University Press.

Laclau, Ernesto and Chantal Mouffe (1987) 'Post-Marxism without apologies.' *New left Review*. No. 166 (Nov./Dec.): 79–106.

Landrum, Nancy Ellen (2000) 'A quantitative and Qualitative Examination of the Dynamics of Nike and Reebok Storytelling as Strategy.' Dissertation, New Mexico State University, Management Department.

Langley, Ann (1999) 'Strategies for theorizing from process data.' *The Academy of Management Review*, 24(4): 691–710.

Lee, S., Courtney, J. and O'Keefe, R. (1992) 'A System for Organizational Learning Using Cognitive Maps', *OMEGA International Journal of Management Science*, 1: 23–36.

Levi, Giovanni (1992) 'On microhistory.' In Peter Burke (ed.) *New Perspectives on Historical Writing*, pp. 93–113. University Park, PA: The Pennsylvania State University Press.

Letiche, Hugo (2000) 'Phenomenal Complexity Theory and Bergson, its Precursor.' To appear in *Journal of Organizational Change Management* special issue on Complexity Theory.

Lucio, Martinez Miguel and Stewart, Paul (1997) 'The paradox of contemporary labour process theory: the rediscovery of labour and the disappearance of collectivism.' *Capital and Class*, 62: 49–77.

Lyotard, Jean François (1979/1984) *The Postmodern Condition*. 1979 is French edition and 1984 is English edition. Trans. By Geoff Bennington and Brian Massumi Minneapolis: University of Minnesota Press.

Madden, Russell (1999) 'Freedom and Causality.' Web document *http://home.earth-link.net/~rdmadden/webdocs/Freedom_and_ Causality.html*

Manning, Peter K. and Cullum-Swan, Betsy (1994) 'Narrative, content, and semiotic analysis.' In Denzin, Norman K. and Lincoln, Yvonna S. (Eds.) *Handbook of Qualitative Research*, pp. 463–483. CA/London: Sage.

Martin, Joanne (1990) 'Deconstructing organizational taboos: The suppression of gender conflict in organizations.' *Organization Science*, 1(4): 339–359.

Marx, Karl (1848) *Manifesto of the Communist Party. Marx/Engels Selected Works*, Volume one, p. 98–137. Mascow, USSR: Progress Publishers, 1969 edition, Translated to English: Samuel Moore in cooperation with Fredrick Engels, 1888. Online Version: Marx/Engels Internet Archive (marxists.org) 1987, 1999, 2000 Transcription/Markup: Zodiac and Brian Basgen *http://www.marxists.org/archive/marx/works/1840/comman/index.html*

Marx, Karl (1867) *Capital: A Critique of Political Economy*. Vol. 1. *The Process of Capitalist Production*. Trans. S. Moore and E. Averling. F. Engles (ed.). New York: International Publishers. First published 1867, English 1967.

McCloskey, Deirdre N. (1998) *Rhetoric of Economics*. (2nd ed.). Madison, Wisconsin: University of Wisconsin Press, 1998.

Mills, Albert J. and Tony Simmons (1995) *Reading Organization Theory: A Critical Approach*. Toronto, ON: Garamond Press.

Mouffe, Chantal (1988) 'Radical democracy: Modern or postmodern?' In Andrew Ross (ed.) *Universal Abandon*, pp. 46–62. Minneapolis: University of Minnesota Press.

Muir, Edward (1991) 'Introduction: Observing trifles.' In E. Muir and G. Ruggiero (Eds.). *Microhistory and the Lost Peoples of Europe*. (pp. vii–xxviii) Translated by Eren Branch. Baltimore/London: The Johns Hopkins University Press. Introduction 'Observing trifles' by Edward Muir.

Muir, Edward and Guido Ruggiero (Eds.) (1991) *Microhistory and the Lost Peoples of Europe*. Translated by Eren Branch. Baltimore/London: The Johns Hopkins University Press. Introduction 'Observing trifles' by Edward Muir.

Mumby, Dennis K. (1987) 'The political function of narrative in organizations.' *Communication Monographs*, 54: 113–127.

Nietzsche, Frederick (1956) *The Birth of Tragedy and The Genealogy of Morals.* Translated by Francis Golffing. New York: Anchor Books (Doubleday). First published 1887.

Nietzsche, Frederick (1967) *The Will to Power*. Trans. Walter Kaufmann and R.J. Hollingdale. New York: Vintage Books.

Peirce, Charles Sanders (1955) *Philosophical Writings of Peirce*. Edited by Justus Buchler. First published in 1940. New York: Dover Publications, Inc. See in particular Chapter 2, 'Abduction and Induction' with writing of Pierce on the topic between 1896 and 1908.

Pepper, Stephen C. (1942) *World Hypotheses: A Study in Evidence*. Berkeley, CA: University of California Press.

Pettigrew, A.M. (1985) *The awakening giant*. Oxford, England: Blackwell.

Pettigrew, A.M. (1990) Longitudinal field research on change: Theory and practice. *Organization Science*, 1: 267–292.

Pettigrew, A.M. and Whipp, R. (1991) *Managing change for competitive success.* Oxford, England: Blackwell.

Pluciennik, Mark, Felipe Criado Boado, Alessandra Manfredini and James L. Peacock (1999) 'Archaeological narratives and other ways of telling/ Comments/Reply.' *Current Anthropology*, Vol. 40(5): 653–678.

Polkinghorne, D. (1988) *Narrative knowing and the human sciences*. Albany: State University of New York Press.

Porras, Jerry (1987) *Stream Analysis: A Powerful Way to Diagnose and Manage Organizational Change*. Reading, MA: Addison-Wesley OD Series.

Powell, Jim (1997) *Derrida for Beginners*. New York: Writers and Readers Publishing, Inc.

Qualitative Solutions & Research Pty. Ltd. (1995) *Nonnumerical Unstructured Data Indexing Searching Theorizing (NUD*IST) [Computer software]. Thousand Oaks, CA: Scolari*.

Richards, Lyn (1999) *Using NVivo in Qualitative Research*. London: Sage.

Ricoeur, P. (1984) *Time and Narrative, Volume 1*, Translated by K. McLaughlin and D. Pellauer, Chicago, IL: University of Chicago Press.

Ritzer, George (2000) *The McDonaldization of Society*. Thousand Oaks, CA: Pine Forge Press.

Rosenau, P.M. (1992) *Post-Modernism and the Social Sciences*. Princeton: Princeton University Press.

Roudiez, L.S. (ed.) (1980) Introduction to Kristeva, Julia 1980 *Desire in Language.* L.S. Roudiez (ed.). T. Gora, A. Jardine and l.S. Roudiez (trans). New York: Columbia University Press.

Schutz, Alfred (1967) *The Phenomenology of the Social World*. Translated by of the Sodal Walsh and Frederick Lehnert. Evanston, IL: Northwestern University Press.

Silverstein, Ken and Alexander Cockburn (1997) (November 16–30) 'Nike's Political Science.' Counterpunch, Vol. 4, No. 20: 1.

Spradley, James P. (1980) *Participant Observation*. New York: Holt, Rinehart & Winston.

Sproull, Lee and Sara Kiesler (1992) *Connections: New Ways of Working in the Networked Organization*. MIT Press.

Stam, Robert, Robert Burgoyne and Sandy Flitterman-Lewis (1992) *New Vocabularies in Film Semiotics: Structuralism, Post-Structuralism and Beyond*. London: Routledge.

Strasser, J.B. and Becklund, L. (1991) *Swoosh: The Story of Nike and the Men Who Played There*. New York: Harcourt Brace Jovanovich.

Summers, D., Boje, D., Dennehy, R. and Rosile, G. (1997) 'Deconstructing the Organizational Behavior Text,' in Special Issue on Postmodern & Critical Theory, *Journal of Management Education*, 21(3): 343–360.

Taylor, Frederick Winsolow (1911) *The Principles of Scientific Management*. New York: W.W. Norton & Co., Inc.

Thatchenkery, Tojo Joseph (1992) 'Organizations as 'texts': Hermeneutics as a model for understanding organizational change.' In W.A. Pasmore and R.W. Woodman (Eds.), *Research in Organization Develop and Change* (Vol. 6, pp. 197–233). Greenwich, CT: JAI Press.

TwoTrees, Kaylynn (1997) Presentation at the International Academy of Business Disciplines conference at Case Western Reserve in Ohio.

Tyler, S.A. (1986) 'Postmodern Ethnography' in Clifford, J. and Marcus, G.E. (Eds.) *Writing Culture: The Poetics and Politics of Ethnography*. Berkeley: University of California Press.

Van Maanen, J. (1988) *Tales of the field: On writing ethnography*. Chicago: University of Chicago Press.

Verena, Stokcke (1992) 'A conquered women,' pp. 55–64. In Yewell, John, Chris Dodge and Jan DeSirey *Confronting Columbus: An Anthology*. Jefferson, NC: McFarland and Company, Inc.

Varner, John Grier and Varner, Jeannette Johnson (1983) *Dogs of the Conquest*. Norman, OK: Unviersity of Oklahoma Press.

Weber, Max (1947) *The Theory of Social and Economic Organization*, tr. Henderson and Parsons. New York: Free Press.

Weber, Max (1958) *The Protestant Ethic and the Spirit of Capitalism*. New York: Charles Scribner's Sons.

Weick, Karl E. (1995) *Sensemaking in Organizations*. Thousand Oaks, CA / London: Sage Publishers.

Weiss, Richard M. (2000) 'What is postmodernism, and what is its potential for the analysis of organizations?' To appear in *Organization Science*.

Weitzman, E. and Miles, M. (1995) *Computer Programs for Qualitative Analysis*. Thousand Oaks, CA: Sage.

Wheatley, M. (1992) *Leadership and the New Science*. San Francisco: Berrett-Koehler.

White, Hayden (1978) *Topics of Discourse*. Baltimore, MD: Johns Hopkins Press.

White, Hayden (1987) *The Content of the Form: Narrative Discourse and Historical Representation*. Baltimore, MD: The John Hopkins University Press.

White, Michael and David Epston (1990) *Narrative means to therapeutic ends*. New York: W.W. Norton & Company.

Wilber, Ken (1996) *A Brief History of Everything*. Boston / London: Shambhala Publications Inc.

Index